GOD

GOD, who are you?
Reflections from the names of God in the Bible.

S. Robert Maddox

REDEFINING Faith RESOURCES

GOD

Published by Redefining Faith Resources

ISBN: 978-0-9890027-9-0

DEDICATION

To all the students in public schools pursuing and engaging in a holistic and healthy education, involving mind, soul and body. Thank you for asking questions on topics teachers normally will not initiate.

There is a GOD!

CONTENTS

FOREWORD

Over the years, it has been a distinct honor to work with many wonderful servant-leaders. Each one along the way has made unique contributions to my life and ministry. The author of the book in hand is one of those individuals. Bob and his wife Brenda bring a certain authenticity to a relationship. Having served alongside them as neighboring pastor, denominational official, and itinerating missionary has given me a multi-faceted perspective of character and competency.

Since a name of God in Scripture is born out of a particular relational experience, it comes as no surprise that my friend Bob would have it in his heart to reflect on God's names. These names are descriptors of the God he knows, loves, and serves. Writing from a reservoir of personal encounters with the Savior, he brings a fresh perspective and a real-life application of what it means to connect with God.

His keen insight and diligent study come together to stimulate the mind, probe the heart, and awaken the spirit. The heart cries out, "Yes, I want to know this God." A spirit of faith rises up and lays hold of the promise that God does not and will not change. Who he was, he is, and evermore will be!

Like those who have gone on before, from the ancient patriarchs, to the early apostles and beyond, let us worship Him, presenting ourselves as a living sacrifice of praise and adoration. Flowing from an all-encompassing worship, we better keep in focus the eternal purposes for our lives.

I appeal to you therefore, brothers, by the mercies of God, to present your bodies as a living sacrifice, holy and acceptable to God, which is your spiritual worship. Do not be conformed to this world, but be transformed by the renewal of your mind, that by testing you may discern what is the will of God, what is good and acceptable and perfect. (Romans 12:1-2)

Thank you, Bob, for helping us get better acquainted with the all-powerful, everywhere present, all-knowing God who exudes unconditional love, incomprehensible grace, and undeserved mercy.

Paul R Martin
Leominster, Massachusetts

PROLOGUE

WHY THE BOOK?

My father drove trains, a tough and rugged occupation. Railroad engineers had to brave avalanche-prone mountain passes and flood-prone lowlands. The railroaders I knew could not create sentences without cuss words, constantly smoked or chewed tobacco, and regularly had alcoholic beverages in their hand. Dad was not comfortable going to church.

My paternal grandfather was also a railroad engineer and one of the first aviators in the Pacific Northwest. After his untimely death, my dad dropped out of high school and worked for the railroad to help support his mother and brother. During the Great Depression, he was laid-off and finished school, receiving a diploma. Rehired by the railroad, he was later drafted during World War II and left a New

York harbor for Europe on Christmas Day, 1944. He drove locomotives in Belgium, transporting troops and supplies. His whole life involved hard work. He finished his 43-year career as the top train engineer in the Pacific Northwest region. He was one of my heroes.

Dad was extremely loyal to the family. My paternal grandmother lived with us throughout much of my growing up years. He was faithfully devoted to my mother and a firm disciplinarian of his kids. You never wanted to cross him and there was little reasoning with him. You simply did what you were told. He raised us to be very independent, think for ourselves, work hard, respect authority, and be responsible for others.

Vacations were great times boating the waters of Puget Sound or camping the wilds of the Canadian Rockies. He was a quiet man who regularly needed personal time and space.

When Dad was in his late forties or early fifties, I came home from school one day and discovered two men visiting with him in the living room. In the kitchen, my mother informed me they were Masons. Apparently, his father had been a member and he always wanted to be one. He went through the initiation steps, becoming a Mason, and eventually a Shriner. This, along with active membership in the

Elks Lodge, was the extent of his religion.

My mother was also from a railroad family. My maternal grandfather was a train conductor for over 50 years, receiving the traditional gold watch. She was even more independent than my dad, rarely depending on anyone for help. It was not unusual to see her tackle a plumbing job or repair an appliance. When Dad was on extended rail trips, she managed the house with a steady hand.

My maternal grandmother died before I was born but may have had a sincere faith in God. Mom grew up active in a Methodist church and later enrolled in a Christian liberal arts college. We attended, and she volunteered, at a local Presbyterian church.

Something happened at the church, causing her to become disillusioned. She continued sending us for a little longer but eventually quit requiring our involvement.

My sister was a sensitive, caring, and compassionate woman. Being the oldest, she had the most religious instruction growing up. She attended Sunday School, learned the stories of the Bible, and earned several certificates and awards. Her attendance at church ended at the end of elementary school. While attending college, her studies brought her to conclude that there is no afterlife. The rest of her years were lived without faith in God and hope for eternity.

My brother was as tough as nails, fearless, and quick-tempered. Following in our father's footsteps, he started very young using foul language, smoking tobacco, and drinking alcoholic beverages. He was forced to attend church, acted poorly in Sunday School, and paid little attention to Bible instruction. To his personal delight, church attendance ended in the middle of his elementary school years. Eventually, his beliefs best lined up with agnosticism—religious existentialism. His search for answers to the mystery of authenticity involved greater knowledge of himself. To him, being certain of a Supreme Being and knowing the ultimate cause was impossible.

Going to church ended for me during kindergarten. I attended very little Sunday School, but occasionally went with a friend to a summer Vacation Bible School. My only recollection of religious instruction was memorizing the Lord's Prayer and the 23rd Psalm, both very dear to me today.

Following my dad's example, I regularly used foul language, began smoking cigarettes at age 10, and drinking beer at 12.

A classmate invited me to her church during my

junior year in high school. The sermon caused me to start searching for God. A couple weeks later, she helped me in her home ask Jesus to become my Lord. I have been living for God ever since.

My history involves secret and social fraternities, Christianity, Atheism, Agnosticism, and following Jesus. Surrounded by such diversity, I had no preconceived notions about a Supreme Being. Raised in an American but not Christian home, my search to understand the God of the Bible was open-face and simple—I just wanted to know Him. Maybe you have found yourself asking, "God, who are You?" The thoughts in this book reflect my discovery.

While reading, keep two things in mind: First, this is about the God of the Bible and a good portion of Scripture is contained in some chapters. Bible passages may be familiar to you but read the verses as well as the narrative. They are designed to blend together.

Secondly, the book is written in a way my father would have understood. I hope everyone enjoys reading these meditations, especially ordinary everyday people.

S. ROBERT MADDOX

INTRODUCTION

WORSHIPERS

I was assigned one day to teach a language class at a public high school, a language I barely know. In each class period, I empowered the smartest language student to present the lesson and to assist struggling classmates; I gave classroom management.

Before the lesson, I briefly spoke about the difference between analytic and agglutinative languages. In one class period, a student raised his hand and asked, "What did you study in college?" I told him my undergraduate study was entitled "Religion and Philosophy", and went back talking about languages.

He raised his hand again. "You have a degree in philosophy? What is your philosophy of life?"

"Are you asking me to tell you *my* philosophy of life?"

"Yeah!"

"You understand that I am not initiating this comment but simply responding to your question."

"Yeah!"

"Class, do you understand that he is asking me to publicly disclose my philosophy of life?"

By this time the whole class was curious, "Yeah! What is it?"

"I can tell you my philosophy of life in four words."

With a smirk on their faces, they murmured, "Yeah, right!"

"Here is my philosophy of life. Are you ready? In four words! Ready? Here it is: (*long pause*) Love God, Hate sin!"

The student asking the question thought for a moment, and finally said, "Cool! I like it."

After the class period, students devoted to Christ

approached to say thanks. They learned a tactic for presenting their beliefs and gained the courage to stand up for their faith in God.

Out of a philosophy of life comes a mission statement. When providing leadership at a Bible College, the institution was upgrading their academic accreditation. The consultant from the accrediting association who was guiding the process encouraged the school to develop a clearer and more concise mission statement. Board members, administrators, faculty, staff, alumni, and various church leaders were asked to contribute. The finished product was a compiling of ideas.

A personal mission statement does not require a committee, but does involve a lot of soul-searching. It can be as tedious as a corporate effort. After much reflection, I developed a four-word personal mission statement: An audience of One!

All my efforts are done for the Lord and are an expression of worship to Him. I appreciate it when others come alongside and take personal ownership of my dreams. I am glad when friends refine my ideas and bring them to a higher level of excellence. I hope others will always benefit from anything championed by me, but my sole focus is God.

Everything is also done for as long as He

determines. A colleague was elected to serve in church denominational leadership but after a few terms was not reelected. He was devastated. A trusted confidant gave him a great word of encouragement: "There is life after serving in elected office. Look for and move on to what God has next." When an activity ends, you can trust Him to lead you to other opportunities.

I have had many meaningful, fulfilling, and wide-ranging opportunities, yet there is always more. What I do, for as long as I do it, is for an audience of One. My life is devoted solely to expressing worship to God.

Worship

Everyone worships something. People easily become captivated by prosperity, personalities, possessions, power, position, and prestige. In this world, many elevate things to a god-like influence. What is worshiped is seen in priorities and lifestyle, coming naturally because people were originally designed to worship the Creator.

The universe reveals a Supreme Being of creative order and infinite variety. Worship is both organized and spontaneous. While worshiping, people become reminded of the greatness and wonder of His majesty. Should adoration become perfunctory, done simply through insincere and hollow activities, comprehension of His vastness and eminence diminishes.

Adulation begins with an awareness of *who* He is, and then moves to appreciation for *what* He does. Since worship is connected to a who question, who is God?

Ask someone following Jesus to describe God and you may hear, "God is love." (1 John 4:8) If given the follow-up question, "What is love?" you may hear, "Love is God!" Although a few people studying Scripture may find this reasonable, answers like these often leave others confused. Furthermore, Bible reading is declining in both society and church; scriptural answers are growing increasingly irrelevant.

What else is said about God? He is a Trinity! What does this mean? The answer usually ends up overly technical. Many following Jesus do not fully comprehend and cannot tell others about His awesomeness.

God is alive, real, and wants a meaningful relationship with you.

When you love the Eternal One, the challenges of life are less overwhelming. When you know the

Supreme Being, the problems being experienced are not amplified out of proportion.

By getting better acquainted with the God of the Bible and recognizing the surpassing value of knowing Him, you can better handle anything life throws at you. A truly amazing God is ready and waiting to help you.

Names

One way to learn about the Lord is by reflecting on the various names and titles given to Him in the Bible. To know a name is to know something special. When people tell you their names, they signal a willingness to know and be known; it is often a prelude to joining their personal journey, an invitation for a relationship.

This is certainly true in Scripture when God chose to reveal His name to people. Some names describe who He is and others describe what He does. Blending these images together gives a clearer picture of the one True God.

What is in a name? Many things! Parents often name a child after someone they love or greatly admire. Children are also given a name because of what it means or how it sounds. My brother gave his youngest daughter the first name "Mercedes" because he liked the sound of it, and the middle name "Maybelle" after someone who deeply influenced his life. Mercedes Maybelle Maddox (MMM) is a *long* name for a beautiful yet *tiny* baby.

In Biblical times, people were named in conjunction with something significant. Newborn Esau was "hairy" and Jacob was "grasping the heel" of his older twin brother at birth. In the same way, the names attributed to God reveals truths about Him and His nature.

God's name, like God Himself, is timeless and unchanging. Although existing outside of time and space, God has revealed Himself in time and space in order to engage people (past, present, and future) in a loving and committed relationship.

So, God, who are You?

S. ROBERT MADDOX

CHAPTER ONE

MERCIFUL

For we ourselves were once foolish, disobedient, led astray, slaves to various passions and pleasures, passing our days in malice and envy, hated by others and hating one another. But when the goodness and loving kindness of God our Savior appeared, he saved us, not because of works done by us in righteousness, but according to his own mercy, by the washing of regeneration and renewal of the Holy Spirit, whom he poured out on us richly through Jesus Christ our Savior, so that being justified by his grace we might become heirs according to the hope of eternal life. (Titus 3:3-7)

I was briefly a member of a singing quartet with the former US Attorney General John Ashcroft. Although I have read his books and heard him speak a couple of times, I deeply appreciated getting acquainted with him. Not only is he an honorable Statesman but a noble Churchman, with an authentic love for the Lord Jesus Christ and the church. He also has a keen sensitivity to the leading of the Holy Spirit.

John developed a presentation based on the 103rd Psalm, incorporating Hymn singing and Scripture reciting. Classic songs of the church were carefully blended into the blessings expressed in the psalm. Not finding suitable music for the phrase, "Who crowneth thee with lovingkindness and tender mercies," he composed, "Yet Still He Crowns Me." The lyrics express how Jesus was given a crown of thorns, but how does He reciprocate? He crowns with loving kindness and tender mercies! Why would He do such a thing?

Years ago, some ministers and wives from Illinois visited New York City to experience Times Square Church, overseen by David Wilkerson. An afternoon was spent in his office in casual conversation. I sat listening as he fielded questions on various topics. Some comments became engraved in my mind, one in particular: he thought living for the Lord would be easier growing older but discovered challenges come at every age. Mercy is a lifetime need.

Aging causes people to reflect on their past.

Reviewing my life, I feel a mixture of gratitude and regret—grateful for numerous opportunities, and regret for moments of selfish behavior. The older I become, the more I realize how dependent I am on God's mercy. God has put up with a lot of my foolishness and stupidity. How does He respond? With a gracious act of kindness! He places a garland of mercy over me.

God is good and generous

The Bible declares that God does not have even a minuscule of evil. Everything He does comes out of goodness. Your good undertakings do not come close to His gracious acts. At no time will God ever be required to say to anyone, "That was a nice thing you did; I owe ya."

A relationship with God is not earned but given. "For by grace you have been saved through faith. And this is not your own doing; it is the gift of God, not a result of works, so that no one may boast." (Ephesians 2:8-9)

Faith is often the emphasis of salvation. Unfortunately, since salvation cannot be gained through massive amounts of kindness, some toil to achieve greater levels of faith. God gives to each person a "measure of faith", sufficient enough to bring them into His saving presence. In reality, eternal life is about grace, with faith simply ushering an individual into His unmerited favor. The focal point of salvation is mercy.

Forgiveness by God is not earned but given. A person naturally wants to make things right when committing a wrong. Although commendable and sometimes required, forgiveness means pardoning and, by its very nature, cannot be deserved.

Hard work often brings promotion. The blessing of God, however, deals with proper standing rather than personal striving. In God's economy, there are no promotions, only positions.

Promotion is about behaving properly to earn esteem. *Position* is about behaving admirably because of association. What believers do is not for gaining eternal life but as an outgrowth of affection. Heavenly status is not merited but given.

Mercy brings a relationship with God

The word *mercy* has several connotations. One Greek word means *kindness or goodwill toward the miserable and afflicted, joined with a desire to relieve it*. Sin causes affliction. An imperfect nature leads to misery. God relieves hopelessness with mercy.

Another Greek word means *the heart of compassion, a manifestation of pity*. Instead of the phrase "heart of compassion," the King James translation uses "bowels of mercy," describing a gut-wrenching feeling. The word also translates as "lovingkindness", an *affectionate kindness produced by deep-felt personal love*.

Mercy involves fondness, kindness, compassion, and pity. Pride often gets in the way of experiencing the benefit of mercy. Prideful people say, "I don't want God's pity. I don't need God's pity." Not true! During a miserable experience, what parent has not taken pity on their child and intervened? God will do no less.

One winter's night in 1935, Fiorello LaGuardia, the irrepressible mayor of New York, showed up at Night Court in a poor ward of the city. He sent the judge home for the night and took over the bench. A tattered old woman, charged with stealing a loaf of bread, appeared before him. Her daughter's husband deserted her and was home sick. The children were starving.

The shopkeeper refused to drop the charges, saying, "It's a bad neighborhood. She's got to be punished to deter further crime."

LaGuardia turned to the woman and said, "I

have to punish you. The law makes no exceptions—ten dollars or ten days in jail!"

While pronouncing sentence, he reached into his pocket, took out a ten-dollar bill and threw it in his hat with these words, "Here is the ten-dollar fine, which I now remit. Furthermore, I am going to fine everyone in the courtroom fifty cents for living in a town where a person must steal bread so that her grandchildren can eat. Mr. Bailiff, collect the fines and give it to the defendant."

The following day, a New York newspaper reported: "Forty-seven dollars and fifty cents was turned over to a bewildered old grandmother. Making forced donations were seventy petty criminals, a few New York policemen, and a red-faced storekeeper."

The Mayor took kindness on someone in misery and combined those feelings with a desire to help. That is mercy!

Knowing you cannot save yourself, God takes pity on you so you will no longer be starving for genuine relationships and eternal life. He sees you unable to adequately do what is necessary to help yourself; not even capable. Out of deep-felt love, He shows mercy by providing the solution. The perfect and good Creator has taken pity on an imperfect and abusive world.

You can do nothing to prove how great you are or how valuable an asset you could be to His kingdom. Self-made righteousness is comparable to the menstrual cloth of a woman, possessing useless and contaminated blood. (Isaiah 64:6) With compassion and mercy, a relationship with God becomes possible by the useful and pure blood of His Son. The blood of Jesus, shed on a cross, cleanses from all unrighteousness.

Recipients of mercy are merciful

How much is a human worth? The individual components of a 150-pound body are worth less than a hundred dollars. An adopted baby can cost $30,000. A kidnapped child may have a million-dollar ransom. God decided you were worth the life of His Son—priceless. You owe a debt to God you cannot pay. As one receiving mercy, reciprocate to others. No one is any worse than the grossness of their own offensive behavior.

For a period of time, I conducted a weekly Bible study in a county jail. Every Friday, prisoners wishing to attend came to the Commons area.

Around this time, a bank president and finance officer were lured to a repossessed farm under the pretense of meeting a prospective buyer. Shortly after arriving, they were ambushed and murdered by the previous owner and son.

During the ensuing investigation, the two murderers were tracked down. A shootout occurred between them and law enforcement. The father was killed, and the son was sent to jail to await trial. He started attending the Bible study.

Unlike many of the regulars, the young man was not big, gregarious, or brutish. He was small framed, reserved, quiet, and unassuming. I discovered three victims were associated with the crime—two bankers and an abused son.

He was rightfully and duly sentenced for his actions and sent to prison. But the defense lawyer, after investigating the tragedy of his upbringing, became deeply moved. He petitioned and received permission to adopt him and started helping him experience a new kind of life, while living with his consequences behind bars.

God thoroughly knows you and is deeply moved by your plight. You have been rightfully sentenced for living a wayward life. The Good News is that He wants to adopt you into his family. The price of His Son pays your debt, and He wants to apply the ransom to your predicament. Will you relinquish any sense of faulty pride and receive the benefit of His mercy?

WHO IS GOD?

Not one thing done by you can gain a better salvation. Eternal life is a gift to all those willing to activate His mercy and call upon the Lord. "Here is God's love, not that you took note of Him, but He took note of you, took pity on you, and gave His Son, because you could not do anything to save yourself." (1 John 4:10, *personally paraphrased*)

God is merciful. Be moved to mercy toward others. Gospel Songwriter Bob Kilpatrick expresses these sentiments in a chorus: "Holy God, make me holy. Merciful God, give me a merciful heart. Lover of souls, help me love them, too, that I might be more like You!" Why not make his thoughts your ambition?

Prayer

Heavenly Father, I recognize my shortcomings and fully understand I well deserve the eternal outcome of my wrongful, unwholesome, and inappropriate thoughts, feelings, and behavior. Thank you for being a merciful God. I come to the righteous Judge and ask that mercy be extended to me.

Thank you, Lord Jesus, for giving Your life that I might experience an eternal relationship with the Heavenly Father. Please apply your remedy to my miserable condition. Cleanse me from my selfish rebelliousness, and cover me with Your selfless righteousness. I devote my life to unreservedly following You.

Thank you for sending Your Spirit to help me fulfill this commitment. Keep me sensitive at all times to His counsel and guidance. Amen.

CHAPTER TWO

MOST HIGH

And Melchizedek king of Salem brought out bread and wine. (He was priest of God Most High.) And he blessed him and said, "Blessed be Abram by God Most High, Possessor of heaven and earth; and blessed be God Most High [El-elyon], who has delivered your enemies into your hand!" And Abram gave him a tenth of everything. And the king of Sodom said to Abram, "Give me the persons, but take the goods for yourself." But Abram said to the king of Sodom, "I have lifted my hand to the LORD, God Most High, Possessor of heaven and earth, that I would not take a thread or a sandal strap or anything that is yours...." (Genesis 14:18-23)

Abram, better known as Abraham, returns to Canaan from Egypt with his nephew Lot, both owning large herds of cattle. Lot goes to the southern region of the Jordan valley, a lush basin, and Abram heads toward the southern hills, a barren wilderness.

A king from the north invades the Jordan valley and travels home with several captives, including Lot and his family. Abram pursues the invaders a long distance and brings everyone back safely. Upon his return two kings greet him—Melchizedek ("righteousness") from Salem, and Bera ("with evil") from Sodom. Abram gives a tithe to the righteous king and takes nothing from the evil one. In the discourse with Melchizedek the name God Most High, *El-elyon*, is mentioned.

Two ancient words refer to God in this narrative. The word "LORD" is *YHWH*, sometimes pronounced *Jehovah*, a Hebraic verb meaning "to be." Centuries later, the same name is passed on to Moses as "I Am," a name giving attention to self-sufficiency, someone not dependent upon anyone or anything. He is self-fulfilled, the perfect fulfillment of all He wills to be, and eternally now, the whole realm of current and all-inclusive time.

The word "God" is an abbreviation of *Elohim*, a plural name possibly referencing the triune God who said, "Let Us make man in Our own image." (Genesis 1:26) The name reflects divine majesty, calling attention to the fullness of power. The word conveys worship of something or someone.

Whenever a manifestation of majestic power occurs worship naturally comes.

In the creation narrative, He is referred to as *Elohim*, the powerful God, and recognized by the balance of nature. Yet He deals with people as *YHWH*, the personable Lord. God is more than a mysterious power; He is the promise-making Lord.

The classic Star Wars series presents the Supreme Being as a force in perpetual conflict with the dark side. Can this bring confusion about the full extent of His nature? Grasping a clear picture of God easily becomes blurred when looking only at *power*. A relationship with God involves recognizing His covenant-making nature, sealing promises by His self-existence.

People make oaths swearing, "So help me God!"—an authority greater than themselves. Nothing is higher than the Lord, and a covenant with Him is binding because of the self-existent "*I Am*!" The Lord keeps agreements as God Most High.

Supreme

In his dialogue with Melchizedek, Abraham discovered that the Lord holds true title to the name God. Despite what someone attempts to make as a god, the Lord is Most High.

The opposite of light is dark. The opposite of up is down. The opposite of day is night. The opposite of God is *nothing*; He is *most* high. No one and nothing is comparably equal.

Through the centuries people have revered various affections and anxieties. Ancient civilizations made gods of the firmaments and celestial formations, nature and earthly creatures, principalities and powers, natural energy and unexplained forces, feelings and passions.

Lessor gods center on positions, possessions, pleasure, and prestige. How many today place careers ahead of principle and materialism above relationships? Anything a person attributes supreme worth towards and allows to dictate their decisions becomes a god. Regardless the object of worship, the Lord is greater.

Those choosing to adore lesser gods are never satisfied with just one. A single god is never enough, yet serving multiple gods leads to destruction. Mythology shows gods competing and attempting to undo each other; destroying instead of creating. The ambition of multiple gods is always annihilation. People living without God Most High experience nothing less than inner turmoil and conflict.

Paul, while visiting Athens, took note of the

numerous monuments made by the superstitious citizens. They made deity of everything, even an "unknown god." He gave a defense for the one True God to the revered scholars of the city. "The God who made the world and everything in it, being Lord of heaven and earth, does not live in temples made by man, nor is he served by human hands, as though he needed anything, since he himself gives to all mankind life and breath and everything. And he made from one man every nation of mankind to live on all the face of the earth, having determined allotted periods and the boundaries of their dwelling place, that they should seek God, and perhaps feel their way toward him and find him. Yet he is actually not far from each one of us...." (Acts 17: 24-27)

No number of shrines will calm the fears of anyone living with many gods. The Psalmist wrote, "For I know that the LORD is great, and that our Lord is above all gods." (Psalm 135:5) God Most High is the only answer.

Supreme perception

"Great is our Lord, and abundant in power; his understanding is beyond measure. (Psalm 147:5)

"I am God, and there is no other; I am God, and there is none like me, declaring the end from the beginning and from ancient times things not yet done…." (Isaiah 46:9-10)

God knows all things, whether they are actual or merely possible, and whether they are pass, present, or future. He knows them perfectly and from all eternity.

This includes people. He knows everyone truthfully and accurately—a source of shame to charlatans and a sense of contentment to the faithful. How futile to be phony with God! No one can be a fake and gain acceptance.

God fully recognizes your feelings, motives, attitudes, thoughts, and desires. He completely comprehends everything associated with you and unconditionally loves you. God is totally aware of every shortcoming and can help you overcome each one.

Supreme power

"All things were made through him, and without him was not any thing made that was made." (John 1:3) God created all things by means of His self-existence.

"For by him all things were created, in heaven and on earth, visible and invisible, whether thrones or dominions or rulers or authorities—all things were created through him and for him." (Colossians 1:16) All created things came out of nothing (*ex nihilo*) and gained substance by Him.

"And he is before all things, and in him all things hold together." (Colossians 1:17) God did not simply fashion the world and then choose to see what became of it. He remains actively involved.

The Lord maintains control of what He crafted and exercises power over circumstances and situations—a source of fear to manipulators and a sense of peace to the exploited.

Supreme presence

"Where shall I go from your Spirit? Or where shall I flee from your presence? If I ascend to heaven, you are there! If I make my bed in Sheol, you are there! If I take the wings of the morning and dwell in the uttermost parts of the sea, even there your hand shall lead me, and your right hand shall hold me. If I say, 'Surely the darkness shall cover me, and the light about me be night,' even the darkness is not dark to you; the night is bright as the day, for darkness is as light with you." (Psalm 139:7-12)

"Am I a God at hand," declares the LORD, "and not a God far away? Can a man hide himself in secret places so that I cannot see him?" declares the LORD.

"Do I not fill heaven and earth?" declares the LORD. (Jeremiah 23:23-24)

No one escapes the presence of God, neither by darkness nor distance. God in His entire being is everywhere—a source of warning to impostors and a sense of cheer to the dedicated.

Whether in a vast ocean or deep cave, God sees. People may try to run away, like the prophet Jonah, but He always knows their location.

While overseeing a church in the northern Black Hills of South Dakota, a good number of members were employed by Homestake Gold Mine. The company provided above ground tours for vacationers. Miners with a perfect safety record, however, could annually invite a couple of friends to tour below ground. One cold January evening, I was one of two guests entering the mines.

Approximately six hundred miles of tunnel lay beneath the town of Lead. I walked through a drift (a vertical tunnel) 8,000 feet below the surface, 3,000 feet below sea level. I saw numerous gold veins along the walls, some a foot wide. Rock temperature is 135 degrees closer to the earth's core. Huge above ground air-conditioners made work possible by forcing surface air into mine shafts, keeping the air temperature at 85 degrees.

Walking through tunnels far below ground got me thinking: does God know where I am? If the battery operating the light on my helmet failed, does He still see me? He knows and sees and is always there.

"Are not two sparrows sold for a penny? And not one of them will fall to the ground apart from your Father." (Matthew 10:29) He even knows the exact hair going down the drain whenever someone shampoos. (Matthew 10:30)

Though evil surrounds and trials assail, God is present. Nothing escapes the notice of the One without barriers and limitations.

During the terrible days of bombing London in World War II, a father holding his son's hand, ran from a building that had been struck. In the front yard was a shell hole. Quickly seeking protection, the father jumped into the crater and held up his arms for his son. He commanded him to jump but the boy replied, "I can't see you!" The father, by the red-tinted sky of the burning building, called to the silhouette of his son, "But I can see you!"

You are able to face life not because you can see but because you are seen, not because you know all the answers but because you are known by God Most High.

WHO IS GOD?

He is El-elyon—God Most High. All-knowing; all-powerful; all-present! He is powerful enough to rule a universe, yet intimate enough to have a relationship with you. He knows everything about you, loves you, and is fully capable of addressing every problem and need.

CHAPTER THREE

EVERLASTING

At that time Abimelech and Phicol the commander of his army said to Abraham, "God is with you in all that you do. Now therefore swear to me here by God that you will not deal falsely with me or with my descendants or with my posterity, but as I have dealt kindly with you, so you will deal with me and with the land where you have sojourned." And Abraham said, "I will swear." When Abraham reproved Abimelech about a well of water that Abimelech's servants had seized, Abimelech said, "I do not know who has done this thing; you did not tell me, and I have not heard of it until today." So Abraham took sheep and oxen and gave them to Abimelech, and the two men made a covenant. Abraham set seven ewe lambs of the flock apart. And Abimelech said to Abraham, "What is the meaning of these seven ewe lambs that you have set apart?" He said, "These seven ewe lambs you will take from my hand, that this may be a witness for me that I dug this well." Therefore that place was called Beersheba, because there both of them swore an oath. So they made a covenant at Beersheba. Then Abimelech and Phicol the commander of his army rose up and returned to the land of the Philistines. Abraham planted a tamarisk tree in Beersheba and called there on the name of the LORD, the Everlasting God. [El-olam] And Abraham sojourned many days in the land of the Philistines. (Genesis 21:22-34)

The journeys of Abraham not only reveal the Lord as *God Most High* but also as the *Eternal God* (El-olam). His timetable is from everlasting, for everlasting, and to everlasting.

After parting company with Lot near the region of the Jordan, Abraham traveled west and eventually arrived at Beersheba, "well of the sevenfold oath." He called upon the everlasting covenant-making God to witness a promise made between him and a Philistine. By invoking the everlasting name, the agreement between the two was to extend beyond their lifetime and considered permanent.

God promises His blessing to everyone who loves and serves Him. For how long? To what extent? Are there time limits? How enduring and unending are they? Is His divine contract with humanity subject to cancellation by Him?

Marriage vows are good for "as long as you both shall live." The Lord, however, makes everlasting oaths.

Everlasting

John starts his gospel narrative by referring to a beginning point, yet the grammatical structure makes the statement unique. The English sentence opens, "*In the beginning* was the Word, and the Word was with God, and the Word was God." (John 1:1) But the original language reads "in beginning"; the article *the* is omitted. The wording suggests, go back to any point called *beginning*, something not possible, and God will be found.

No starting point marks the beginning of God. He is *from* everlasting. Never has there been a time when He did not exist. People have a creation moment, a conception. The commencement of living is celebrated with a *birthday*. Christmas is sometimes referred to as a birthday but is actually the Incarnation. Jesus already existed and simply came in bodily form.

God is also *to* everlasting, without end. "The LORD will reign forever and ever." (Exodus 15:18)

He not only *exists* but *reigns* for eternity. No one will ever usurp, eliminate, or replace Him. No one is strong enough, smart enough, or deceitful enough to remove Him from His throne.

World rulers come and go but the Lord will rule *forever*. He is, therefore, deserving of everlasting honor. "But the LORD is the true God; he is the living God and the everlasting King." (Jeremiah 10:10)

Prominent dignitaries receive honor as long as they govern, and are occasionally remembered and appreciated beyond their life. But God is the Ruler every leader is subservient to, the Sovereign One of eternal splendor and admiration. "To the King of the ages, immortal, invisible, the only God, be honor and glory forever and ever." (1 Timothy 1:17)

"Have you not known? Have you not heard? The LORD is the everlasting God, the Creator of the ends of the earth. He does not faint or grow weary; his understanding is unsearchable." (Isaiah 40:28)

People sometimes become exhausted and tired in their ongoing toil and efforts. The Everlasting Lord never becomes drained or grows fatigued while reigning over the universe. He does not become fed up with problems or bored with situations, nor will He discard anyone like an old toy. God is tirelessly everlasting.

Everlasting precepts

Many mistakenly assume eternal life begins at death; someone is said to have entered eternity after leaving this life. Living in time without end, however, starts the moment faith is placed in God. He shapes everlasting life in everyone following Jesus.

Abundant life is a relationship with the Everlasting Lord as guided by His everlasting precepts. (John 10:10) Bountiful living became established in eternity and is seen by living according to the pattern of His word. (Joshua 1:8) He is presently transforming believers into the image and likeness of His Son. By walking in the Spirit, life becomes abundant.

Studying the Bible and gaining honorable behavior is critical. "All Scripture is breathed out by God and profitable for teaching, for reproof, for correction, and for training in righteousness." (2 Timothy 3:16) The precepts of God first bring you down and condemn you, *then* pick you up and establish you.

Before entering Air Force basic training, I thought I did a good job caring for myself. Then I met Tech Sergeant Cash. For weeks, he told the barracks we did everything wrong. He spent every day, all day, yelling: "You don't shave right; you don't brush your teeth right; you don't shine your shoes right; you don't clean and press your clothes right; you don't eat right; you don't talk right; you don't walk right."

The Flight became very discouraged and ended up feeling, "What's the use?" He then started building us back up, teaching proper hygiene, nutrition, physical conditioning, dress, posture, and mannerism. When finally established as highly skilled Airmen, he gave us permission to be called "Cash's Tigers." A sense of worth and invincibility soon followed. Boot camp became profitable in reestablishing our lives in a more satisfying way.

The everlasting Word of God starts by disclosing everything about you is all wrong. It speaks bluntly about being sinful, full of transgressions. It then teaches the right way to think, feel, and behave. You become established in the pattern of eternal living and clearly identified with the name of the Lord.

Cultural standards are inconsistent; social trends come and go; life is full of highs and lows. Fads pass, but God's word is faithful, constant, and true. "God is not man, that he should lie, or a son of man, that he should change his mind. Has he said, and will he not do it? Or has he spoken, and will he not fulfill it?" (Numbers 23:19)

Basing behavior upon circumstances is faulty. To live a stable life, sane life, and satisfying life requires something unchanging. Situations inevitably fluctuate and you need guidance by a source from everlasting, for everlasting, and to everlasting. While facing countless changes, center your response on the changeless Word of God. Scripture can straighten out a life going in circles. "The grass withers, the flower fades, but the word of our God will stand forever." (Isaiah 40:8)

Everlasting patience

The Lord has desired a relationship with you from eternity. "I have loved you with an everlasting love; therefore I have continued my faithfulness to you." (Jeremiah 31:3)

"The Lord is not slow to fulfill his promise as some count slowness, but is patient toward you, not wishing that any should perish, but that all should reach repentance." (2 Peter 3:9)

Jesus could have returned for His church ages ago. Throughout the centuries more than enough wrongful behavior has occurred in this world. He could have said at any time, "The world overflows with cruelty and corruption; I will put an end to it!" Yet He prolongs His return, wanting more people to change their mind and come to Him.

His everlasting word not only declares everlasting patience, but also an everlasting promise—His imminent return. Very soon the One knowing everything will conclude, "The Kingdom is complete. I'm coming back!" His everlasting word states that today is the day of salvation; now is the acceptable time.

One month too late: At a prayer meeting in western Washington, a young man was feeling convicted about his lifestyle. People asked if he wanted to have a relationship with God. He hesitated, and said, "I have another month of hauling logs, then I'll decide." Four weeks to the day, he was swimming in Lake Lacoma, got a cramp, and drowned. He was one month too late.

One week too late: A woman in Scotland became troubled about her spiritual condition. After walking the floor most of the night, she wrote in her diary, "Next week, I will attend church and make things right with God." The next day, she went to a wild party, took violently ill, and became delirious for about a week. Before her death, the delirium left long enough for her to reportedly say, "I'm lost!" She was one week too late.

One day too late: At a church service, a young lady was urged to put her faith in God. She said she would make things right tomorrow. The following day, her mother discovered she intended to spend the night carousing and pleaded with her not to go. She replied, "I am going even if I die!" and went to dress. No reply came from her room when a friend came to pick her up. Her mother went to check and found her dead. She was one day too late.

One hour too late: A teenager in New York attended church with her parents. An aunt confronted her about her relationship with God. She refused to listen. At the close of the service, they started home. There was an accident and she was thrown violently against a telephone pole, dying instantly. She was one hour too late.

The Lord waits for you, but you do not know how much more time you can wait. No one knows when Jesus will come, or when they will receive their final summons. Decide!

WHO IS GOD?

He is El-olam—the Everlasting God. He invites you by His everlasting word to experience the promise of an everlasting life. He is everlastingly patient, but declares that today is the day for entering into a meaningful relationship with Him.

CHAPTER FOUR

PROVIDER

When they came to the place of which God had told him, Abraham built the altar there and laid the wood in order and bound Isaac his son and laid him on the altar, on top of the wood. Then Abraham reached out his hand and took the knife to slaughter his son. But the angel of the LORD called to him from heaven and said, "Abraham, Abraham!" And he said, "Here I am." He said, "Do not lay your hand on the boy or do anything to him, for now I know that you fear God, seeing you have not withheld your son, your only son, from me." And Abraham lifted up his eyes and looked, and behold, behind him was a ram, caught in a thicket by his horns. And Abraham went and took the ram and offered it up as a burnt offering instead of his son. So Abraham called the name of that place, "The LORD will provide" (Jehovah-jireh); as it is said to this day, "On the mount of the LORD it shall be provided." And the angel of the LORD called to Abraham a second time from heaven and said, "By myself I have sworn, declares the LORD, because you have done this and have not withheld your son, your only son, I will surely bless you, and I will surely multiply your offspring as the stars of heaven and as the sand that is on the seashore. And your offspring shall possess the gate of his enemies, and in your offspring shall all the nations of the earth be blessed, because you have obeyed my voice." (Genesis 22:9-18)

My wife and I are grandparents. We have fantastic grandkids—beautiful and handsome, smart and witty, loving and charming, daring and adventuresome. Their amiable personalities compel us to give lots of hugs and kisses. They are a special joy. We usually see their very best qualities and send them back to mom and dad for any necessary discipline and correction.

Occasionally, they wear us out. Raising small children is designed for younger adults; older people are better at lending counsel, encouragement, and temporary assistance.

The birth of a couple grandchildren was touch and go. Their conception and pre-natal were a challenge, causing many anxious moments. Much time was invested in prayer. Their birth brought a sense of relief. All of them are healthy and full of life.

Abraham, in his old age, was given a promise of a child, Isaac. The boy was an important part of the everlasting covenant. Through him would eventually come the One able to restore a meaningful relationship with the one True God. Yet, Isaac became the focal point of a great test for Abraham, a test of love and loyalty. Now that he received the promised child, was God still Most High? Had his devotion weakened, diminished, or faded away?

Much was asked of this worn and weathered man. How could a loving dad even consider taking the life of a son, especially someone conceived in the most impossible of situations? The mandate would be hard enough for someone young but devastating for someone near the end of life.

Abraham laid his son on a makeshift altar, extending a knife over his vital organs. At the last possible moment, a voice from heaven shouted, "Stop!" A ram, caught in a thicket, was sacrificed in his place. A substitute sacrifice was given on Mount Moriah, just as the divine Substitute took your place at nearby Mount Golgotha. An offering was required and Jehovah-jireh provided.

[Choruses and songs use the more familiar English

name Jehovah, causing me to occasionally use the name in place of YHWH]

The significance

Jehovah-jireh means, "the Lord sees." The Old English word *provide* best describes the connotation: "pro" means "beforehand", and "vide" (contained in the word *video*) means "to see." The Lord foresees, or sees well in advance.

God provided in advance a specific place for Abraham to give sacrificial worship. There are seven mounds around Moriah, modern-day Jerusalem. The father and son were directed to a specific mountain where the Lord provided a ram caught in a thicket. The One who foresees made divine arrangements for the sacrifice.

People become frightened about unforeseen situations, worried and upset when not understanding what is happening. God's answer for anxiety is, "I know what is coming and have already provided for you." As there was a ram waiting for Abraham, God has a provision waiting for you, whatever the need.

After overseeing a church in southwest Minnesota for five years, an invitation came to pastor in the northern Black Hills of South Dakota. The church had been in existence for seven years, growing quickly, but later experiencing financial difficulties. They fell behind in land and building payments, and owed money to several merchants in town. I was asked to become the new pastor and help them experience a financial turnaround.

Going to the merchants, I apologized on behalf of the church for the past-due bills and made a commitment to fully pay them within 30 days. I stated future purchases would be strictly cash and carry. One merchant responded, "You've got that right!" Serious public relations problems were confirmed.

I went to the landowner holding the Contract for Deed and told him payments would resume immediately. I went to the finance company holding a note on the building and promised payments would resume in 30 days.

Everyone accepted my plan. The congregation gave sacrificially and generously. The Lord miraculously helped.

The leadership council of the church initially offered an adequate salary, plus benefits. Six weeks after arriving, my wife and I knew the church could not afford the financial arrangements. At the next leadership meeting, I informed them of a personal decision to take a pay-cut and to suspend benefits. To supplement personal income, I asked if they would be comfortable with me driving a school bus during the early mornings and late afternoons. Recognizing the unfortunate situation, they reluctantly agreed.

Our youngest son had a chronic problem with tonsils, experiencing regular sore throats and fevers. The situation deteriorated to the point that just three days without an antibiotic caused a relapse. Although no longer commonly practiced, the doctor advised removing the tonsils.

Without health insurance, the doctor gave permission for monthly payments. I also made financial arrangements with the hospital. Our son was scheduled for surgery the following Monday. I brought my wife and son to the hospital, did my school bus route and returned. The surgery went well.

No one in the congregation was told about the situation or the need. The people were doing great helping the church financially. My wife and I felt this was a family matter. We would privately deal with the problem.

Churches, back then, annually gave an expression of appreciation to their pastor—gift certificate at a nice restaurant, a small gift, cards and letters, or a special reception with cake and coffee.

Having heard about the voluntary pay-cut, the congregation secretly planned to take up a collection for us during the annual emphasis.

The special offering was done the day before the tonsillectomy and presented to us in the church service. When the medical bills arrived, the amount received covered the total cost of both the doctor and hospital, to the exact dollar.

"I have been young, and now am old, yet I have not seen the righteous forsaken or his children begging for bread." (Psalm 37:25)

"Bless the LORD, O my soul, and forget not all his benefits ... who satisfies you with good so that your youth is renewed like the eagle's." (Psalm 103:2, 5)

The Lord sees well in advance and makes provision for when you arrive.

The stipulations

Provisions are not automatic. Three ongoing expressions seen in Abraham, recognized as the friend of God, reveal how to divinely receive the necessities of life.

The Lord provides when there is unwavering faith. "You have obeyed me." (V. 18) Faith becomes sight by carrying out the commands of God.

Abraham obediently went to the hills of Moriah and faithfully brought Isaac with him. What if he had chosen just any mountain instead of the one selected by God? Would the divine provision have been wherever he chose to go? Unwavering faith caused him to explicitly fulfill the instructions and experience the blessing.

After sensing a divine call into church ministry, I planned to leave the Air Force at the end of my enlistment and attend college. I had done well in the military, was promoted at minimum time-in-grade, and received a fairly good income. But my wife and I decided to make a transition to Northwest University at Kirkland, Washington.

As the date of my discharge drew closer, we were expecting our first child. The Air Force had offered me a generous reenlistment bonus. At the same time, a major aircraft manufacturer in Seattle had lost a few sizeable contracts, laying off thousands. The region was going through a deep economic recession.

My first instinct, as a soon-to-be father, was to continue serving in the military. Another thought was to attend college in a different part of the country, where the economy was better. Even though fearfully wondering about the right decision, we relocated to Washington with our few modest possessions.

I went searching for a job. The Job Placement Service just received an employment notice from a major bank as I was filling out the necessary paperwork. I went immediately for an interview and was offered a job that worked perfectly with my class schedule.

The God who foresees made provision. Had I wavered and failed to act, the provision would have been there, but someone else would have been the recipient.

The Lord provides when there is unconditional love. Abraham was being tested with the question: Was the Lord above all other relationships? Did Abraham allow his love to transfer from God to a child of blessing? The challenge is still being given today.

God delights in giving. He is the greatest Giver. His joy is in showering believers with blessings. If not careful, you may stop gazing at His eyes and start gawking at His hands. Lovers watch eyes; beggars search hands!

Are you a lover enamored by the Giver? Or have

you become a beggar captivated by a gift?

Abraham regularly demonstrated love for God by faithfully giving offerings, but did he have *unconditional* love? Would he give up his most prized gift? You must answer this question, as well.

The test of unconditional love normally involves a precious item, something or someone held onto tightly. Divine provisions become jeopardized when an object or person is considered more important than God.

The Lord provides when there is undeniable hope. Abraham had a great promise: From Isaac would come a great nation. Was the lad now supposed to be a sacrifice? The father of faith had a hope in resurrection power. Should death be required, God would raise him from the dead!

"By faith Abraham, when he was tested, offered up Isaac, and he who had received the promises was in the act of offering up his only son, of whom it was said, 'Through Isaac shall your offspring be named.' He considered that God was able even to raise him from the dead, from which, figuratively speaking, he did receive him back." (Hebrews 11:17-19) Abraham rested on an undeniable hope of God's death-defying power.

"So when God desired to show more convincingly to the heirs of the promise the unchangeable character of his purpose, he guaranteed it with an oath, so that by two unchangeable things, in which it is impossible for God to lie, we who have fled for refuge might have strong encouragement to hold fast to the hope set before us. We have this as a sure and steadfast anchor of the soul, a hope that enters into the inner place behind the curtain." (Hebrews 6:17-19)

WHO IS GOD?

He is Jehovah-jireh—the Lord your Provider. The Lord foresees and makes a way. With unwavering faith, unconditional love, and undeniable hope, you can experience divine provisions.

S. ROBERT MADDOX

CHAPTER FIVE

ALMIGHTY

The LORD said to Moses, "Now you shall see what I will do to Pharaoh; for with a strong hand he will send them out, and with a strong hand he will drive them out of his land." God spoke to Moses and said to him, "I am the LORD. I appeared to Abraham, to Isaac, and to Jacob, as God Almighty (El-Shaddai), but by my name the LORD I did not make myself known to them. I also established my covenant with them to give them the land of Canaan, the land in which they lived as sojourners. Moreover, I have heard the groaning of the people of Israel whom the Egyptians hold as slaves, and I have remembered my covenant. Say therefore to the people of Israel, 'I am the LORD, and I will bring you out from under the burdens of the Egyptians, and I will deliver you from slavery to them, and I will redeem you with an outstretched arm and with great acts of judgment. I will take you to be my people, and I will be your God, and you shall know that I am the LORD your God, who has brought you out from under the burdens of the Egyptians. I will bring you into the land that I swore to give to Abraham, to Isaac, and to Jacob. I will give it to you for a possession. I am the LORD.'" (Exodus 6:1-8)

Life is filled with problems. You would think by growing older, after experiencing numerous difficulties, obstacles, and setbacks, tribulations would not cause alarm. The fact is, the older you get the better you understand the magnitude of the challenge and sometimes end up feeling more overwhelmed. The struggles of life can leave people greatly beleaguered, requiring them to continually remember that battles belong to the Lord and are never too big for Him.

The divine name recorded in this narrative is El-Shaddai and is connected to freedom, delivering Israel from Egypt. The book of Exodus is a testimony of His unlimited ability to set captives free.

The word *shaddai* comes from the root word "shadad", meaning to *deal violently, to devastate, to ruin, or to destroy.* God vehemently destroys anything causing enslavement and bondage to those loving Him. In the New Testament, He is referred to as Almighty only in the last book—Revelation, the record of final retribution.

The term first appears in Genesis 17, when God entered a covenant with Abraham. He attaches the full might of His glory to the establishment of divine promises, and exercises His infinite capacity to redeem covenant-makers from any and all oppression.

If God knew Israel would eventually become enslaved to Egypt, why did He send them there in the first place? As a protective act! Canaan, the crossroad and trade route of the world, constantly attracted conflict. In Egypt, the *family of Jacob* could safely develop into the *tribe of Israel* while under the protective power of a strong nation. After Israel became a *nation within a nation*, the Almighty God dealt with the mighty Egyptians for mistreating the Hebrews and fulfilled a longstanding promise.

Shaddai is primarily about *sufficiency*. Moses said, "I am insufficient; use my brother Aaron." God responded, "I am all-sufficient; I will be with you."

The people wondered, "How can slaves be victorious over a mighty army?" God declared, "The Lord Almighty will fight the battle."

God is sufficiently able to defeat the enemies of

his purposes and bring victory to his people. He is infinitely capable of exercising liberating might for those who love and serve Him.

Here are three areas where God shows supreme sufficiency.

All sufficient over sin

The word *sin* speaks of a rebellious and imperfect nature, and is the biggest problem anyone will ever face. Romans 3:23 is undeniably true: "All have sinned and fall short of the glory of God." No one is without defect in heart, mind, and body. No one lives perfectly.

Bondage to Egypt is considered a *type* (similar in characteristic) to loose-living and waywardness. As Israel was enslaved to Egypt, everyone is enslaved to sin. Jesus said, "Truly, truly, I say to you, everyone who practices sin is a slave to sin." (John 8:34) Israel experienced redeeming might and you, in your situation, can as well.

Living for centuries in Egypt, the people of Israel had become comfortable in slavery. But when Pharaoh hardened his heart toward them, they wanted to be set free. Similarly, the vast majority of people today are comfortable in sin. When they begin to experience the ramifications of sin, they come to desire freedom.

The full blessing of liberating might cannot be experienced when someone is content in enslavement. The purpose of redeeming power is freedom.

No one experiences the supremacy of El-shaddai who is happy in sin. No one experiences the benefits of El-shaddai who debates the need to separate from selfishness, materialism, and individualism. When brought to a place where you are no longer secure in your sin and desire to be set free from its bondage, you discover the full scope of El-shaddai.

God is all-sufficient to deal with the effects of sin. He removes guilt through repentance, transforms shame into forgetfulness, and converts wickedness into righteousness.

"As far as the east is from the west, so far does he remove our transgressions from us." (Psalm 103:12) On this planet, you can go only so far north before heading south and so far south before going north. However, you can go west continuously and east without interruption. The redeeming might of the Lord over your transgression is as limitless as east and west.

He is the Almighty God, able to effectively deal

with your sin.

All sufficient over diseases

"If you will diligently listen to the voice of the LORD your God, and do that which is right in his eyes, and give ear to his commandments and keep all his statutes, I will put none of the diseases on you that I put on the Egyptians, for I am the LORD, your healer." (Exodus 15:26)

Diseases commonly occurred among the Egyptians. By living like them, Israel could expect much of the same. If they paid attention to God, they could avoid many infirmities, illnesses, and ailments. Not only is God mighty to *deliver*, but He is able to *prevent*.

Harmful behavior becomes a major source of diseases. People become ill by careless living—improper diet, lack of exercise, inadequate rest, chemical addiction. Unwholesome living insults and mistreats freedom.

Strained relationships, refusing to forgive, and bitterness of heart, can also cause illnesses. Wrongful attitudes rob peace of mind, causing physical tolls. Some healings are linked to pardoning and taking on a different outlook.

Many conditions are resolved by lifestyle decisions. Devotion to God, integrity, and clean-living, can prevent many health issues.

My brother died in 1997, the day before Thanksgiving. We were very close growing up, roommates for my first sixteen years. I am extremely thankful he was my brother and loved him very much. Unfortunately, we shared some harmful habits.

My brother and I served in separate branches of the Armed Forces during the Vietnam War. In 1965, he entered the U.S. Army; in 1967, I enlisted into the U.S. Air Force. In 1966, between these two enlistments, I became a member of the Lord's army.

Scripture, the spiritual warfare training manual, tells the troops to follow the Captain of the Heavenly Host and not be dominated by enemy forces. Eventually, the Supreme Commander instilled in me the strength to give up a couple life-controlling and physical-threatening addictions.

After our discharges from military service, we once again spent time together. The relationship between us became impacted by a spiritual gulf. We deeply cared for each other, but lifestyles had become radically different. Eventually, separate career paths caused us to live in distant locations from each other.

The last extended period together occurred when a very loving and caring step-grandmother died. The week became very traumatic. While making the final arrangements at a funeral home, our mother experienced a major stroke and became hospitalized. My brother drove home from Montana and I flew in from North Dakota to attend the memorial service and set up mom's rehabilitation.

While in Seattle, we stayed in our childhood home. On the morning of the funeral, I was eating breakfast in the kitchen while my brother was showering in a nearby bathroom. His hacking and coughing lasted over five minutes. I told him of my concern. He stated this occurred every morning.

If I had not become a follower of Jesus, this could have been me. Obedience to God kept me from mornings of uncontrollable coughing. His prevention instructions will also keep you from various diseases.

All sufficient over enemies

Living among enemies is a major topic in Exodus. The Egyptians had become unbearable taskmasters, no longer giving useful service to God and His plan. The living conditions had become deplorable. Israel cried out to God and His liberating might dealt decisively with them.

After decades of church ministry, I am perceived a friend by some and an enemy by others. Talking about spiritual matters can cause either hunger, or anger. Although the truth can set people free, some are not ready to hear the truth—just ask Moses. Doing anything consequential for God in a corrupt world will create enemies.

Scripture is crystal clear: The Lord never desires for you to take matters into your own hands. When people have something against you or wish you harm, the Lord does not help those who help themselves.

As followers of Jesus, there is no room for revenge or its attributes—a critical attitude or cynical spirit. Possessing a *get even* mentality is proof of personal deficiencies and shortcomings, limiting the benefits of liberating might.

God wants to "bring you out from under the yoke." He desires to "free you from being slaves." He wishes to "redeem you with an outstretched arm and with mighty acts of judgment." This includes freedom from feeling a need to settle scores. When payback is pursued at home, at work, at school, or even at church, a failure occurs in recognizing the Lord as El-shaddai.

There is no room in a godly heart for sarcasm, cynicism, or reprisal. Enemies are His problem and He is responsible for dealing with them.

Years ago, I met an amazing man by the name of Doyle Thompson. Prior to becoming a pastor, he was a non-commissioned officer in the Air Force and a decorated war hero. Since I was a young Airman planning to spend a lifetime in church ministry, he took a special interest in me. I enjoyed our numerous conversations.

Doyle was recovering from an illness at an airbase hospital and I went to visit him. During our chat, he talked about a situation that occurred in his military career. A certain officer did not like him and, solely on account of this person, Doyle was overlooked whenever his name came up for promotion. This became a prolonged injustice. He was deprived of a well-earned advancement.

In his heart, Doyle knew the Lord would deal with the matter. As it turned out, he became slotted to receive a special medal of commendation. Standing before the entire squadron, with many high-ranking officials present, that very man was required to present the medal. Shortly afterward, the officer received orders to relocate.

Doyle sensed this was God's way of making

things right. He counseled me, "Don't worry about those who want to harm you. Keep your heart right."

Are you experiencing the heavy hand of disparagement, defamation, or disdain? Stand behind the shield of the Lord! He is your shelter.

WHO IS GOD?

He is El-shaddai—God Almighty. He mightily conquers transgressions, illnesses, and adversity.

S. ROBERT MADDOX

CHAPTER SIX

HEALER

Then Moses made Israel set out from the Red Sea, and they went into the wilderness of Shur. They went three days in the wilderness and found no water. When they came to Marah, they could not drink the water of Marah because it was bitter; therefore it was named Marah. And the people grumbled against Moses, saying, "What shall we drink?" And he cried to the LORD, and the LORD showed him a log, and he threw it into the water, and the water became sweet. There the LORD made for them a statute and a rule, and there he tested them, saying, "If you will diligently listen to the voice of the LORD your God, and do that which is right in his eyes, and give ear to his commandments and keep all his statutes, I will put none of the diseases on you that I put on the Egyptians, for I am the LORD, your healer (Jehovah-

rapha)." (Exodus 15:22-26)

Previously, brief attention was given to preventing diseases. But what is known about healing and the Healer, *YHWH-rapha*?

God sufficiently addresses both sin and sickness. The Great Physician made provision for healing in the redeeming work of Golgotha. Complete restoration is at the core of salvation.

Should an infirmity occur while living uprightly, the Lord can graciously cure the malady.

Plans for healing

The Egyptian medical journal *Ebers Papyrus* was written in 1552 BC, around the time Moses was born. Hundreds of remedies were advised. Potions included such things as dust of a statue, shell of a beetle, head of an electric eel, guts of a goose, tail of a mouse, fat of a hippopotamus, hair of a cat, eyes of a pig, toes of a dog, milk of a woman, semen of a man.

For graying hair: "To prevent the hair from turning gray, anoint it with the blood of a black calf which has been boiled in oil, or with the fat of a rattlesnake."

For hair loss: "When hair falls out apply a

mixture of six fats, namely those of the horse, the hippopotamus, the crocodile, the cat, the snake and the ibex. To strengthen, anoint with the tooth of a donkey crushed in honey."

For snakebites: "Give them magic water to drink." (Water poured over a specific idol.)

For embedded splinters: "Apply worm's blood and asses' dung." (Animal waste is loaded with tetanus spores. Lockjaw took a heavy toll of splinter cases.)

Moses was a Hebrew growing up in the royal court and educated in Egyptian wisdom. He was acquainted with the medical knowledge of his time. Hebrew slaves also knew and may have practiced some of the common remedies.

Israel left Egypt with a different health plan, one with a promise. The *plan* was to "listen carefully to the voice of the LORD your God...do what is right in his eyes...pay attention to his commands...keep all his decrees." The *promise* was twofold: There would be "none of the diseases", and "I am the LORD, who heals you"—either prevention or cure.

God did not promote or advance the medical practices of that era. The Egyptian-educated Moses was divinely challenged to place unwavering faith in a divine prescription. Had he faltered, the first five books of the Bible, the Pentateuch, may have included something like, "the tooth of a donkey crushed in honey."

What does the heavenly plan include?

First, *keep His commandments*. Failing to abide in obedience and failing to use common sense is a major source of health issues.

For years, I suffered each winter from severe sore throats. Someone told me that wearing a hat when the temperature was below 40 degrees Fahrenheit would greatly reduce head colds and throat inflammation. I have not had a major issue since.

A friend went overseas to do ministry in a part of the world where women regularly carry large and heavy bundles on top of their head when transporting goods down the road. At the end of every church gathering, he would invite anyone wanting prayer to come to the front of the auditorium. Women regularly requested prayer for aches and pains in their neck. If they changed the way they hauled cargo, the problem would be greatly reduced, or probably not exist.

My children came to me with injuries of ankles,

knees, elbows, and wrists. While examining the wounded joint, they would attempt to move it for me and say, "It hurts when I do this!" Before giving serious attention to the problem, I would jokingly respond, "Then don't do it!" My humor was often not appreciated at the moment, but how many people are doing things harmfully impacting good fitness?

Scripture counsels to live in ways reducing the potential of poor health. Following His counsel and taking simple precautionary steps can do much to improve physical wellbeing and greatly reduce some of the more common ailments.

Secondly, *be more concerned about walking with God then being cured.* Everyone wishes relief from suffering and the effects of physical restrictions. The challenge is living above whatever afflictions life throws at you.

Ailments can become excuses, causing uncalled for limitations. Numerous blind, deaf, amputee and paralyzed people have made their handicaps bridges instead of barriers. They made necessary adjustments and created strengths out of perceived weaknesses. Many restrictions are more an issue of mind and heart than of body.

In a few situations, an infirmity actually gave an advantage. Sing the songs of the blind songwriter

Fanny Crosby and you gain a clearer vision of His majesty. How many blind people see God better than those with excellent eyesight?

Mary Reed was a missionary to India. While on furlough, the American doctors discovered leprosy. She decided to return to India to spend the rest of her days as a leper ministering to lepers. In answer to prayer, she was healed and for over 20 years continued her fruitful life among the sufferers of this disease.

At the same time, another missionary contacted the same disease on the same mission field. Although much prayer was offered for his healing, Mr. Davis continued to have leprosy. He lived such a life of spiritual victory that he perhaps blessed more people than if he had been healed. Dictating a letter to a friend when his feet and hands were nearly gone, his sight and hearing impaired, and his voice only a whisper, he said, "If I had a voice, I would be singing all day long."

Which glorifies the Lord more, a fit body or robust soul? The center of life is God. Focus more on serving than suffering. Healing has more to do with wholeness than health.

Kinds of healing

Volumes have been written making healing appear as simple as one, two, three. A few authors have suggested fulfilling divine rules and principles makes healing a *done deal*. Really?

Jesus, in His earthly ministry, demonstrated variety in healings: blind eyes restored by placing mud on them; a physical condition addressed by touching a garment; a disease cured by fulfilling specific instructions. He was physically present for some healings and visibly absent from others. The only thing consistent with healing is the Healer.

Scriptures testify of healing for body, heart, and soul.

Healing of the body. Illnesses and handicaps can be divinely healed. Luke testifies of a high fever braking (Luke 4:39); someone paralyzed, lowered through a roof, gaining mobility (Luke 5:18-25); leprosy, the most dreaded disease of the ancient world, being cured (Luke 5:12-13); a deformed hand becoming fully functional (Luke 6:6-10).

Healing of the heart. The Lord can heal hurt feelings and emotional wounds. He can heal the trauma of natural calamity and physical duress. He can bring peace and rest to a turbulent heart.

Job developed a bitter heart, wrongly accusing God of a cruel fate and ravaged body. The Lord corrected the heart condition, challenging him to possess an accurate outlook and to live humbly, leading to complete renewal.

Healing of the soul. A tormented soul usually becomes manifested as depression. Melancholy often comes as a frontal attack against a relationship with God. After amazing acts of supernatural power, a person can become extremely despondent.

The older covenant prophet Elijah, after experiencing and witnessing mighty manifestations of God, went through a severe depression. (1 Kings 18-19) At a mountaintop experience, he called fire down from heaven. He immediately descended to the stream of reckoning, destroying falsehood. He quickly ascended the hilltop of prayer, birthing a rain cloud on the western horizon. He swiftly ran miles in the valley of decision, confronting corruption. All in one day!

He experienced a series of successes, was emotionally pumped, and riding a spiritual high. While all this was occurring, he gave little attention to the tenuous physical and mental malady developing within. Any personal rejection would be catastrophic, and Queen Jezebel provided the catalyst.

He needed a nap, nourishment, and nudge. The Lord prodded him in a gentle breeze, a barely detectable force that takes longer to bring results. You may not always sense Him moving you forward, but progress occurs even when barely noticed. Depression is not out of His healing reach.

For every kind of agony, there is a divinely designed antidote. No unhealthy condition is out of reach of the Healer.

Source of healing

Healing, by the nature of things, is unpredictable. Grace is involved. The nine grace actions of the Spirit, recorded in First Corinthians 12, refer to eight manifestations as "gift" but the manifestation of healing as "gifts." There are pluralities of healing.

All healing is from the Lord. Scientists marvel at the resiliency of the human body. God created a body capable of curing.

What do surgeons do? They cut, clean, remove, or replace, then close an incision. The muscles, tissues, organs, and ligaments do the restoring and mending. God deserves full honor for what a divinely created body can do.

Sometimes people exhaust every possible means and then say, "It's up to the Lord now. There is nothing more we can do." To make Him the last option is a mistake.

Get God involved right away. James instructs, "Is anyone among you sick? Let him call for the elders of the church, and let them pray over him, anointing him with oil in the name of the Lord." (James 5:14)

You must call for prayer. Asking others to petition the Lord is your act of faith. Those praying are expressing faith by talking to God on your behalf. Expecting the Lord to mysteriously drop your need into the mind of others does not line up with Scriptural instructions.

While overseeing a church in Minnesota, a man was dying from Parkinson's disease. I would regularly visit him on Tuesday afternoons. During one of my routine visits, I discovered he was near death. I asked his daughter, "Why didn't you call?" She said, "I just knew if the Lord wanted you here, He would lay it on your heart." What sometimes sounds spiritual is more mystical than Biblical. Faith that is full gets others involved.

WHO IS GOD?

He is Jehovah-rapha—the Lord your Healer. Young children go to their parents when sick. As a follower of Jesus, you are a child of God. Come to your Heavenly Father when in need of healing. He has healing power available for you.

S. ROBERT MADDOX

CHAPTER SEVEN

VICTOR

Then Amalek came and fought with Israel at Rephidim. So Moses said to Joshua, "Choose for us men, and go out and fight with Amalek. Tomorrow I will stand on the top of the hill with the staff of God in my hand." So Joshua did as Moses told him, and fought with Amalek, while Moses, Aaron, and Hur went up to the top of the hill. Whenever Moses held up his hand, Israel prevailed, and whenever he lowered his hand, Amalek prevailed. But Moses' hands grew weary, so they took a stone and put it under him, and he sat on it, while Aaron and Hur held up his hands, one on one side, and the other on the other side. So his hands were steady until the going down of the sun. And Joshua overwhelmed Amalek and his people with the sword. Then the LORD said to Moses, "Write this as a memorial in a book and recite it in the ears of Joshua, that I will utterly blot out the memory of Amalek from under heaven." And Moses built an altar and called the name of it, The LORD Is My Banner [Jehovah-nissi], saying, "A hand upon the throne of the LORD!" (Exodus 17:8-16)

Washington DC is full of war monuments, helping the nation remember brave moments of the past. While visiting the capital, my wife and I went to see the displays for World War II, the Korean Conflict, and the Vietnam War.

The Vietnam Memorial was personally heartbreaking. There are 58,272 names inscribed on black marble. Some represent wives and children forever waiting back home. Others signify girlfriends suspending plans to marry. Every name embodies the love of moms and dads.

A close friend, killed in combat, has his name on the Wall. Another classmate committed suicide shortly after returning to the States, unable to live with his war experiences and battle wounds. A life-threatening chemical used in the jungles during my brother's tour of duty shortened his lifespan. He died before our mother did. The first thing mom said to me afterward was, "It's not supposed to happen this way. Parents should go first!"

I served on the island of Okinawa from the middle of 1968 to the end of 1969. The present-day conveniences of communication did not exist at the time. Service personnel overseas had little knowledge of the chaos starting to destroy the heart and soul of America. Information was strictly filtered, carefully worded in the Stars and Stripes newspaper and selectively reported on Armed Forces radio. Letters from home were positive and upbeat, mostly about family.

The war produced public scorn and ridicule, not ticker-day parades. Many soldiers, airman, and sailors became angry over the mistreatment experienced upon their return. No matter where someone served overseas, unfounded name-calling and senseless accusations had to be often overlooked by those fortunate enough to get back safely. Upon arrival at the San Francisco International Airport, everyone traveling in military uniform (as required) was thought to be a "baby killer."

Shortly after returning stateside, I went to a local food store. The checkout clerk was a former high school classmate. She asked what I had been doing. I replied, "I've just returned from overseas duty." The young man bagging groceries overheard the comment and made a derogatory remark.

She was very familiar with my behavior prior to

following Jesus. Although converted, I was not completely sanctified. The guy looked grateful when she quickly wedged herself between us. He almost went through the front window.

The American military won every skirmish in Vietnam but lost the war. There was no victorious banner, mostly bewilderment, confusion, and misunderstanding.

The Star-Spangled Banner, written by Francis Scott Key on September 14, 1814, was written after seeing the U.S. flag at Fort McHenry withstanding a night long bombardment from an offshore British warship. The first stanza reads: *"Oh say, can you see, by the dawn's early light, what so proudly we hailed at the twilight's last gleaming, whose broad stripes and bright stars, through the perilous fight, over the ramparts we watched, were so gallantly streaming? And the rockets' red glare, the bombs bursting in air, gave proof through the night that our flag was still there...."* The raised standard declared the nation was not defeated.

Yet, the lyrics end with the ultimate question: *"...Oh, say, does that Star-spangled Banner yet wave, O'er the land of the free, and the home of the brave?"* The jury is still out! Someday, the history books will record the final verdict.

If a national flag waves high on a battlefield, the enemy has not overpowered the encampment. Similarly, Moses lifted his hands like a banner for the Captain of the Heavenly Host. As long as his arms were extended upward, the people witnessed victory.

When the skirmish was over, a monument was built in a barren battlefield for *YHWH-nissi*—the Lord our Banner. He alone was the banner under which Israel successfully rallied. The memorial represented the triumphant Victor. Stones erected in the wilderness gave both encouragement and a challenge: memories of the enemy will one day end; and never forget the One who truly conquers.

Some of the worse battles occur when spiritually dry and wandering aimlessly to no particular place. How does someone gain victory when encountering unexpected and difficult trials? How does a person get through barren moments, especially when hindered by the enemy of their soul?

Follow the instructions

Consider the description of the scene, slightly paraphrased:

"Moses, Amalek is coming to fight My people."

"Lord, what am I to do?"

"Quickly get up the hill and raise your arms."

Running away could easily be perceived as cowardice. Raising arms could be misunderstood as surrendering. God's way may appear unreasonable, but any divine strategy requires diligent obedience.

Upon entering Canaan, the tactic against Jericho was equally confusing:

"Lord, should we build ramps along the wall and prepare for a long siege?"

"Nah, just walk around the place every day and it will be over in a week."

When Amalek was approaching, the conscientious leader Moses most likely planned to get involved on the battlefield. The result would have led to defeat. Only when faithfully following divine guidance can supernatural victory be experienced. When Moses was unable to fulfill the special instructions, when he could no longer keep his arms up, the battle went against them.

The Christmas season in my older years is much less hectic and more peaceful. "Peace on earth" has finally arrived in the celebration. Occasionally, I miss the assembling of toys done as a young father. Each of the four kids wanted their gifts assembled first and fast.

If the assembly appeared obvious, instructions were not read. If the constructed toy did not look or do as stated on the box, I hunted discarded wrappings for directions.

Presently, the Lord is assembling your life, making you completely and fully functional. As you journey with Him to your final inheritance in Christ, sometimes through dry and barren moments, carefully follow divine instructions and experience victory.

Accept help and support

Part of my military basic training taught the correct way to enter into formation—how to line up equally spaced and straight. The left arm was extended out, touching the shoulder of the person on the left. The head and eyes faced the opposite direction, lining up straight with those on the right. When the squadron was correctly positioned, the drill instructor would command, "Ready, front!" The left arm went down, the head faced forward, and everyone stood at attention.

Usually, the last command came quickly. Sometimes, as an endurance test, the sergeant would not give the final order, leaving the left arm painfully extended. As limbs grew heavy, arms started dropping, causing additional drills and conditioning.

Moses' arms grew increasingly tired. When he was unable to keep them up, Aaron and Hur gave aid.

God places you in a community of believers for this very reason. You are surrounded by friends, serving as modern-day Aarons and Hurs. Does someone need to be giving you some solid support right now?

Moses could have said to his brother and friend, "I will do it my way; I don't need anyone's help!" Yet, everyone would have suffered. Refusing help not only hurts you but also the very purpose of God.

"If one member suffers, all suffer together; if one member is honored, all rejoice together." (1 Corinthians 12:26)

You have asked Jesus to be the absolute Leader of your life, but you cannot successfully accomplish this without the help of others. You alone must lift up the Lord to experience victory, but you cannot adequately keep Him raised by yourself.

Faith in God means *community*. No one fully develops faith on their own. Your life will occasionally need encouragement so that you and others following Jesus can experience complete victory.

Scripture describes Moses as the meekest (humblest) man on earth. Pride keeps believers from the benefit of help. Any inability to accept assistance serves as a warning of unwholesome arrogance.

An office picture became popular years ago that showed a turtle sitting on top of a fence. The caption read, "If you see a turtle on a fencepost, you know he had some help." Whenever you think, "Wow, this is marvelous what I've done!", ask yourself: How can a turtle get on top of a fence post?

You will only be successful to the level that you allow others to get involved.

Let God work

When assembling toys at Christmas, my children often liked to watch. If they became extremely fascinated with the process, they sometimes would block my view, stopping the work.

Are you doing the same with God? Move out of the way so He can bring the victory. What the Lord does is always fascinating, but is He being hindered by you?

Some mistakenly believe they must help God when they ask Him to take care of a problem. If things do not develop as they hoped, they step in.

Trust Him and stand *behind* His banner. Choosing to take charge makes divine victory impossible.

The leader Moses seriously bore his duties and responsibilities, yet Israel would not have experienced victory had he stepped in and taken over. He stood aside and witnessed supernatural results. You must do the same.

The best thing you can do in spiritual battles is stay out of the way. Stand clear and give the Lord working space. Scripture declares every battle is His. He triumphs best without interference.

Thank the Lord

Moses ended the battle by building an altar. He stopped and expressed appreciation to God.

Faithfully attending worship gatherings is how you stop and thank God for victory. Give time to building a memorial of praise with others; uphold an attitude of gratitude!

Most people I know dislike being taken for granted. Do you like it when others just expect you to do something? Do you want to get involved when they just assume you will? Probably not! Then why do the same with the Lord?

Build an altar of thanksgiving! Always be

grateful to God for the victories of life.

WHO IS GOD?

He is Jehovah-nissi—the Lord our Banner. Follow His instructions, accept help, allow Him to work, and thank Him. Whatever the situation, victory is divinely possible.

S. ROBERT MADDOX

CHAPTER EIGHT

PEACE

Now the angel of the LORD came and sat under the terebinth at Ophrah, which belonged to Joash the Abiezrite, while his son Gideon was beating out wheat in the winepress to hide it from the Midianites. And the angel of the LORD appeared to him and said to him, "The LORD is with you, O mighty man of valor." And Gideon said to him, "Please, sir, if the LORD is with us, why then has all this happened to us? And where are all his wonderful deeds that our fathers recounted to us, saying, 'Did not the LORD bring us up from Egypt?' But now the LORD has forsaken us and given us into the hand of Midian." And the LORD turned to him and said, "Go in this might of yours and save Israel from the hand of Midian; do not I send you?" And he said to him, "Please, Lord, how can I save Israel? Behold, my

*clan is the weakest in Manasseh, and I am the least
in my father's house." And the LORD said to him,
"But I will be with you, and you shall strike the
Midianites as one man." ... Then Gideon perceived
that he was the angel of the LORD. And Gideon said,
"Alas, O Lord GOD! For now I have seen the angel
of the LORD face to face." But the LORD said to
him, "Peace be to you. Do not fear; you shall not
die." Then Gideon built an altar there to the LORD
and called it (Jehovah-shalom), The LORD Is Peace.
(Judges 6:11-16, 22-24)*

One way to study a person recorded in Scripture
is by creating a personality profile. There are
primarily four personality types: two naturally
extroverted and two innately introverted. Everyone
is a combination and blending of all four traits yet
one, sometimes two, dominate.

The outward types either initiate purpose or
initiate people. Prominent leaders and trendsetters
usually have these personalities.

The inward types either respond to purpose or
respond to people. Highly creative, or those
preferring a support role, or people wanting to work
behind the scenes normally have these personalities.

The extroverts are generally bolder, more
adventuresome, and greater risk-takers. They are

comfortable being in control and embrace change as a way of life.

The introverts are normally more analytical, methodical, and steady. They are innovative, imaginative, resourceful, inventive, and artistic, working best in changeless environments.

When moved out of their comfort zone, outward people can quickly react with anger; inward people guardedly struggle with fear.

What was Gideon like? Where was he when the Lord appeared to him? Hiding in a winepress, yet doing something defiant. His bold actions were discreetly done.

Reading the rest of his record shows someone struggling with doubt, feeling inadequate, second guessing directions, and questioning personal competence. He regularly needed affirmation and special confirmation. He hesitantly took charge in critical situations and had little ambition to rule over others.

His tendencies were dominantly *inward*, though possessing a couple of outward inclinations. He generally does not fit the personality of a world changer. What better way for the Lord to demonstrate supernatural power than to select someone lacking the drive and ambition to be famous and prominent?

Gideon the fearful (v. 11)

Gideon was beating grain in a winepress, but God addresses him as a mighty warrior.

A winepress during this period was not large or something someone could easily hide in. The scene is a contrast of actions—hiding and defying, clandestinely beating grain.

Beneath the anxiety of getting caught was a heart of valor. What he was doing was a clear act of boldness. Gideon was someone who recognized an injustice and acted, despite his fear. He may have been hiding, but he was doing something courageous.

When Gideon was confused about the national state of affairs and fearful of getting caught in a covert operation, *YHWH-shalom* appeared to him.

Gideon the fretter (v. 13)

Gideon fretted between what he was seeing and what had been told him. "Why has all this happened to us? Where are all Your wonders that our fathers told us about? Did not the one True God bring us out of Egypt?"

None of these questions offended the Lord, yet none were answered by Him either. No explanation would have brought personal satisfaction. God appeared to Gideon because *His presence* is the answer to every question.

My book <u>SPIRIT Living</u> ends with a story that helps clarify this truth. When overseeing a church in a northwest suburb of Chicago, an older gentleman was actively involved. We occasionally golfed together. Even in his eighties, he played a great game. Riding together in a golf cart, he would tell fascinating stories of an Italian Pentecostal church he attended while growing up in the city.

Becoming increasingly ill, he realized his time on earth was coming to an end. His departure to be with the Lord was soon coming. During a hospital visit, I found him in a public seating area deep in thought. I quietly sat next to him and asked what was on his mind. He told me about a troubling dream he had the night before.

Jesus appeared, standing in front of him, lovingly looking at him. He started asking questions about his life; things he had been wondering about for a very long time. Jesus simply stood there without making a comment or giving an answer.

"What do you think this means?" he asked.

I replied, "Jesus does not just give answers—He is the Answer! To every question, God offers Himself as the solution."

The explanation to the frightening moments of life is a loving relationship with God, not knowledge. Insight about every circumstance you experience will never bring personal peace and contentment.

Gideon had wondered if the people of Israel had done something to cause this oppression. Was something hindering God's intervention? Good question!

Earlier the narrative records, "I said to you, 'I am the LORD your God; you shall not fear the gods of the Amorites in whose land you dwell.' But you have not obeyed my voice." (Judges 6:10)

The first thing Gideon did, after encountering God, was destroy idol worship. "When the men of the town rose early in the morning, behold, the altar of Baal was broken down, and the Asherah beside it was cut down, and the second bull was offered on the altar that had been built." (Judges 6:28) He returned God to His rightful place and YHWH-shalom responded with deliverance.

What idols are hindering God from being the answer to your need? His peace is revealed when He is loved with a whole heart.

Gideon was fretting and his heart was void of peace. Are you fretting over your situation?

Psalms 37 instructs, "Do not fret because of evil men.... Trust in the LORD and do good.... Commit your way to the LORD.... Be still before the LORD and wait patiently for him.... do not fret—it leads only to evil.... For evil men will be cut off."

To every challenge of life, the Lord is your peace.

Gideon the frightened (v. 15)

Gideon was instructed to rescue the people from oppression. He considered himself the least qualified for the assignment—the least member, of the least family, of the least tribe of Israel.

When the Lord was looking for a viable candidate, Gideon thought God had reached down into the bottom of the barrel—no social status, no educational standing, and no financial prominence.

Gideon was anxious, frightened, and totally inadequate. The Lord, however, knew exactly what he was capable of doing.

Many wonderful things are learned when being

the least. God is rarely seen in self-achieved fame, but always shines in humility. God is often not recognized among those with personal strengths, but is clearly witnessed in weakness.

Inadequacy can work to your favor, causing you to lean more on God and staying totally dependent on Him. When fright rules and peace vacates, YHWH-shalom wants an audience with you.

Gideon the ferocious (v. 23)

Whether caused by fear, fret, or fright, God can make a difference. Are you depressed while sitting in your winepress of confusion? Are you anxious about the direction your life is taking? Are you developing an ulcer on account of what needs to be done?

Listen carefully and hear the Lord say deep within your soul, "Peace! Do not be afraid." (v. 23)

How strange for followers of Jesus to lack peace. He said, "My yoke is easy; My burden is light." Carefully line up with His will, closely attach yourself to Him, and fully depend on His strength. He is your rest.

Scripture gives wonderful promises:

"For to us a child is born, to us a son is given; and the government shall be upon his shoulder, and his name shall be called Wonderful Counselor, Mighty God, Everlasting Father, Prince of Peace." (Isaiah 9:6)

Jesus said, "Peace I leave with you; my peace I give to you. Not as the world gives do I give to you. Let not your hearts be troubled, neither let them be afraid." (John 14:27)

Paul wrote, "For He himself is our peace...." (Ephesians 2:14)

Peace is not found a place but a Person.

The Lord is peace

Jerry Graham accidentally discovered at age 8 he was an illegitimate child and felt unwanted. By 14, he was jailed for chronically running away. By 19, he experienced incarceration *where flies do not land*—solitary confinement. He considered himself State raised.

For 24 years, he was in and out of jails and penitentiaries—a dope addict, pimp, and thief. At 38, he was labeled a habitual criminal, meaning life imprisonment. He was hardened, profane, and hate-filled.

The loving concern of someone following Jesus pierced his hardened heart. In a cellblock, he found the Prince of Peace. Even though the consequences of his way of life did not change, he was content.

A poem was written about him:

> Today I went into a prison
> Where I looked on anguish and strife
> But the message I learned from a convict
> I'll remember the rest of my life.
>
> The prisoner said he was content
> In paying society's due.
> "It's easy to render to Caesar," he said,
> "when you have the Master with you."
>
> I've seen his anger fly out of hand
> For he was just human, you see
> Then ask both offended and God to forgive
> Unashamed – when bending his knee.
>
> Many long years it has been since I had
> The faith that this convict has shown
> And though I was with him for only a while
> His message has pointed me home.
>
> Yes, today I went into a prison
> And saw there to my disbelief
> The face of our Savior Lord Jesus
> Worn on the face of a thief.

Having faith in God does not always change circumstances, but forever transforms a countenance.

WHO IS GOD?

He is Jehovah-shalom—the Lord is Peace. During fear, fret, and fright, God is your peace.

The Hebrew word "shalom" means *completeness, soundness, welfare, peace*. He is contentment and completeness in every circumstance.

(Acclaimed Books, Dallas, TX: <u>Where Flies Don't Land</u>, by Jerry Graham and M.L. Johnson, 1977)

S. ROBERT MADDOX

CHAPTER NINE

RIGHTEOUSNESS

[Referring to the King] *"Behold, the days are coming, declares the LORD, when I will raise up for David a righteous Branch, and he shall reign as king and deal wisely, and shall execute justice and righteousness in the land. In his days Judah will be saved, and Israel will dwell securely. And this is the name by which he will be called: 'The LORD is our righteousness.'"* [Jehovah-tsidkenu] (Jeremiah 23:5-6)

[Referring to His kingdom] *"Behold, the days are coming, declares the LORD, when I will fulfill the promise I made to the house of Israel and the house of Judah. In those days and at that time I will cause a righteous Branch to spring up for David, and he shall execute justice and righteousness in the land.*

In those days Judah will be saved, and Jerusalem will dwell securely. And this is the name by which it will be called: 'The LORD is our righteousness.'" [Jehovah-tsidkenu] (Jeremiah 33:14-16)

When the movie "The Lion, the Witch, and the Wardrobe" was released to theaters, I made mention of it in a Sunday morning service. A very upset mother approached me afterward, angry for publicly endorsing the film. She was not allowing her children to see it because a witch is included in the story. She wanted to know how a Christian minister could justify approving something involving an evil being.

I responded, "To gauge something, there must be a measurable standard. You understand good by comparing it with evil. The word *genocide* is somewhat vague until you mention Adolf Hitler. The term is better understood when personified in someone attempting to exterminate a group of people with biasness and prejudice. To accurately assess the actions of the virtuous lion, evil was personified in a witch, helping both the book and film communicate the subject of redemption."

The Apostle Paul wrote to Roman believers that the pure, holy, and divine Law of God makes transgressions and wrongdoings clearly known. Once Law was given, sin became measurable.

The Hebrew word *tsidkenu* is about justice and rightness. Living right *should* be normal, but what is right? How is a just standard established? Better yet, who determines an honest and true paradigm?

The justice code of the United States is rooted in the Ten Commandments. Why did this become the yardstick? Because these directives were proven reliable in earlier civilizations and, more importantly, they came from the Creator of mankind.

When a person or a group of people design their own standard, everything becomes negotiable; nothing is clearly right or wrong. For *everyone* to be treated fairly and equally, a suitable pattern of behavior must come from a greater source. How foolish to measure yourself by yourself!

Years ago, a well-known conservative congressman was gaining national approval for his political agenda, causing major stirrings among more liberal lawmakers and news sources. A television news commentator interviewed his very elderly mother. The conversation was fairly uneventful until asked what she knew about her son's personal opinion of the President. The mom was unwilling to comment until deceived.

The reporter kept prodding her and finally said, with a twinkle in her eye and smile on her face, "It will just be between you and me." The microphone was still held by her mouth. To the delight of the commentator and television network, the fairly popular President was poorly portrayed. The broadcast came off as an aggressive attack against the congressman and his popular plan.

The viewing audience reacted harshly toward the shoddy tactic. The commentator promptly justified her actions as an acceptable practice for gaining news. Yet, if she was willing to trick an inexperienced elderly woman to obtain comments, what stopped her from deceiving the nation when giving reports?

She and the television network became branded as a biased news source and lost viewers. They thought their actions right, but the public considered them dishonest and morally deficient. They mistakenly measured themselves by themselves, a faulty standard.

Human nature is vulnerable to rebellion and pride. For there to be a community, or even a civilization, people cannot establish their own righteousness. Self-righteousness generally leads to harm and unwholesome outcomes.

If you cannot establish your own righteousness, you cannot create your own eternity. No one can achieve heaven on their own. People are powerless to rightfully attain a dwelling place with God. Everyone needs a relationship with *YHWH-tsidkenu*, the Lord our righteousness.

Those believing in Jesus are found in Him not having a righteousness of their own but the righteousness from God that comes through and is dependent upon faith. (Philippians 3:9)

Righteousness defined

Righteousness, as a basic literal meaning, is *being in the right*, and is not connected to majority opinion. No matter the size of opposition, even if standing alone, a person can still be right. A majority may enact laws, but being right is not an enactment.

When my children were growing up, it never settled well with me if they attempted to justify behavior by saying, "But everyone is doing it." They would quickly receive my impersonation of the Fonz, from the television sitcom "Happy Days", embellishing the word "Soooooooo!"

The weakness of a democratic society is found in the question, "Can the majority be wrong?" Yes! Generally, men and women are more prone toward being self-focused, egotistical, and deceitful.

Jesus spoke in the Sermon on the Mount about the road being wide that leads to destruction. What caused the width to be broad? Was it built wide? The original language suggests the path was not *designed* wide but *became* wide by extensive use, by the high volume of traffic.

Being right is not based on the size of a crowd but on the infallible standard of God. Governments and corporations can be destroyed when lawmakers or business associates perceive themselves right solely by joining others and blindly following a charming but wayward leader.

Righteousness is a legal matter, associated with pardoning and parole. Pardon is received with an acknowledgment of guilt; parole is given when transgressions are admitted. When someone concedes their nature is faulty and asks God to forgive, He pardons and renders them acquitted. Righteous is the person who receives the divine verdict of blameless.

Living in God's righteousness means being forgiven the debt of sin, declared clean, and now standing in upright truth.

Righteousness displayed

God is the fountain of truth. Everything He does

is just and right. He is never unfair. When the floods came in the days of Noah, the Lord acted justly. When fire and brimstone came upon Sodom and Gomorrah, He acted rightly.

Abraham said about God, with regards to Sodom, "Far be it from You to do such a thing, to put the righteous to death with the wicked, so that the righteous fare as the wicked! Far be that from You! Shall not the Judge of all the earth do what is just?" (Genesis 18:25)

Followers of Jesus are not part of the final Great White Throne judgment. Why? Because He rewards the righteous but judges the wicked.

Out of His righteousness comes vindication for His people. Retribution is an element of divine justice. "God considers it just to repay with affliction those who afflict you, and to grant relief to you who are afflicted…." (2 Thessalonians 1:6-7)

Liberate yourself with this thought: You never need to harbor ill-will or resentment. God deals with every injustice. In Christ, you are set free from things making others bitter and vengeful. His reputation in Scripture is of rescuing, vindicating, and demonstrating, through the outcome of events, that those who love Him are right. God righteously addresses every issue His people face.

The history of oppression and deliverance in Scripture reveals the righteousness of God. Rescuing Israel from Egypt is described as His righteous deeds (1 Samuel 12:7). Pharaoh referred to the plagues as evidence of the rightness of God: "Then Pharaoh sent and called Moses and Aaron and said to them, 'This time I have sinned; the LORD is in the right, and I and my people are in the wrong.'" (Exodus 9:27)

During the period of Judges, liberating acts were described as righteous. Deborah, in her song of deliverance, sang, "You who ride on white donkeys, you who sit on rich carpets and you who walk by the way. To the sound of musicians at the watering places, there they repeat the righteous triumphs of the LORD, the righteous triumphs of his villagers in Israel." (Judges 5:10-11) Victory validated that Israel was right.

Restoring the people of Israel from exile shows His righteousness: "I bring near my righteousness; it is not far off, and my salvation will not delay; I will put salvation in Zion, for Israel my glory." (Isaiah 46:13) By Hebrew captives returning to the Promise Land, their right standing with God was revealed.

The righteousness of God is now available through Christ: "For I am not ashamed of the gospel, for it is the power of God for salvation to everyone who believes, to the Jew first and also to the Greek.

For in it the righteousness of God is revealed from faith for faith, as it is written, 'The righteous shall live by faith.'" (Romans 1:16-17) Though not in the majority, when living as a follower of Jesus, you are in the right.

Righteousness demands

What does abiding in the righteousness of God expect of you? Simply this: Never take matters into your own hands. Let Him reveal His righteousness in you. Allow Him to be your Vindicator.

"Beloved, never avenge yourselves, but leave it to the wrath of God, for it is written, 'Vengeance is mine, I will repay, says the Lord.' To the contrary, 'if your enemy is hungry, feed him; if he is thirsty, give him something to drink; for by so doing you will heap burning coals on his head.' Do not be overcome by evil, but overcome evil with good." (Romans 12:19-21)

Rendering kind and honorable behavior to those mistreating you creates in them a facial complexion like the amber of burning coals, a look of shame and embarrassment.

Nowhere in scripture will you read life is fair. Everywhere in the Bible you have the promise of God being faithful.

Are you refusing to rest until grievances are dwelt with? Are you failing to trust in God's faithfulness?

Charles H. Spurgeon, the great English orator, wrote: "God abides in faithfulness. He is faithful in *love*. He knows no variableness, neither shadow of turning. He is faithful in *purpose*. He does not begin a work and then leave it undone. He is faithful in *relationships*. As a Father, He will not renounce His children. As a Friend, He will not deny His people. As Creator, He will not forsake the work of His hands.

"He is faithful in His *promises* and will never allow one of them to fail to a single believer. He is faithful to His *covenant*, which He has made with us in Christ Jesus and ratified with the blood of His sacrifice. He is faithful to *His Son* and will not allow His precious blood to be spilled in vain. He is faithful to *His people* to whom He has promised eternal life and from whom He will not turn away.

"This faithfulness of God is the foundation and cornerstone of our hope. He continues to keep His people and therefore they continue to keep His commandments."

King Saul unjustly and vehemently pursued David, the righteous warrior. Freedom from the jealous king would eventually come, but not quickly.

When given an opportunity to murder Saul, David refused to take matters into his own hands. Loyal friends even suggested God arranged the entrapments for the very purpose of ending the king's life, but David believed it was not right to take advantage of vulnerable moments. As he maintained a right heart, the day of divine deliverance came. He stood upon God's promises.

Leave every injustice with the Lord and stand in His righteousness.

WHO IS GOD?

He is YHWH-tsidkenu—The Lord our righteousness. He deals justly with the injustices of life. Abide in His righteousness and place greater confidence in Him.

S. ROBERT MADDOX

CHAPTER TEN

PRESENT

These shall be the exits of the city: On the north side, which is to be 4,500 cubits by measure, three gates, the gate of Reuben, the gate of Judah, and the gate of Levi, the gates of the city being named after the tribes of Israel. On the east side, which is to be 4,500 cubits, three gates, the gate of Joseph, the gate of Benjamin, and the gate of Dan. On the south side, which is to be 4,500 cubits by measure, three gates, the gate of Simeon, the gate of Issachar, and the gate of Zebulun. On the west side, which is to be 4,500 cubits, three gates, the gate of Gad, the gate of Asher, and the gate of Naphtali. The circumference of the city shall be 18,000 cubits. And the name of the city from that time on shall be, The LORD Is There. [Jehovah-shammah] (Ezekiel 48:30-35)

Ezekiel was the son of a priest and likely a priest

himself. He was taken from the land of Israel and relocated near the river Chebar. At approximately thirty years of age, his ministry began, lasting twenty-two years. He gave a comforting message to those held captive in Babylon.

His prophecies demonstrated God was perfectly justified in permitting captivity. In fact, the Lord was acting mercifully. Instead of destroying Israel, as done to nations committing similar abominations, He dealt correctively with them. Ezekiel instructs the people of Israel to make the necessary adjustments required by captivity, sustain faith in God during their exile, and expect divine restoration one day.

The departure of God's glory, described in Ezekiel 10 and 11, is critical to the prophetic message. The Glory first leaves the Most Holy Place, moving to the threshold of the Temple. The Glory then departs from there and rests on an angelic throne-chariot. A cherub moves the Glory to the east Temple gate, before leaving the area altogether. Finally, the Glory abandons Jerusalem and comes to rest on the Mount of Olives.

God left because of sin and idolatry, yet left reluctantly and gradually. The last thing the Lord wants to do is leave. He departs slowly. He hopes people notice His presence is not where it once was or where it is supposed to be. In other words, His presence is not *there,* and they should seek to restore Him to His rightful place.

Is it any different today? His departure from wayward followers of Jesus is never abrupt and immediate. He leaves little by little with hope they will sense He is missing and seek to restore Him to the rightful place.

As chapters 10 and 11 show God progressively departing, chapter 43 gives an awe-inspiring vision of His mercy and grace filling the temple once again. With the return of Glory, the captive priest residing near the river Chebar has a vision of a life-giving river coming from His dwelling place. The water grows in depth and width, providing life and fruitfulness to everything it touches.

The climax is a promise that God will live eternally with His people. The prophetic word ends with the pronouncement: "The Lord is there!"

What is the priestly prophet saying about *YHWH-shammah*? The essence of joy is having the Lord in your life, having the Lord *there*. His presence sweeps away sorrows, disappointments, and heartaches. If willful and wrongful actions produce consequences of disgrace and shame, His transforming Spirit can create a course correction and restoration.

Why should anyone desire and seek a return to God? Because life is more rewarding when He is there!

Where is the Lord presently residing in your life? Is He in the center of your activities and associations? Has sin and idolatry caused a distance to occur? Has He been marginalized, pushed to the threshold or the gate? Worse yet, has He been relegated outside?

When people in a relationship with God ignore Him, He attempts to correct rather than condemn, but wayward behavior and indifference can eventually cause consequences. What kind of captivity will be required of you to once again experience YHWH-shammah, the Lord is there?

Four experiences often cause people to question His presence.

Times of trouble

Troubles cause feelings of aloneness. Caught up with worry and fear, people struggle sensing God is there.

One trip to Israel included going to Hebron, the place where David first reigned as king and the site of the Patriarch's Tomb—the burial cave of

Abraham and Sarah, Isaac and Rebecca, Jacob and Leah. To finally see the second most sacred site in the Holy Land was inspiring, something I have wanted to do for years.

While going through the mountainous region, we entered very dense fog. Trouble is similar to traveling and suddenly coming upon a thick mist. You know a highway is ahead, but all you see are the road markings directly in front of you. The way is there but the fog hinders your ability to see. When trouble comes, everything becomes clouded and you wonder, "Is God there?"

The psalmist wrote out of a momentary fog, "Why, O LORD, do you stand far away? Why do you hide yourself in times of trouble?" (Psalm 10:1)

When overseeing a church in Minnesota, events were regularly scheduled during winter to minimize cabin fever, unhealthy feelings associated with prolonged isolation and enclosed settings. A volleyball game was scheduled one frigid night at a High School gym, five miles from town. Several families attended.

While there, an unexpected snow blizzard hit. We immediately formed a caravan and headed back to town. The weather was severe, the vehicles were spaced 5 to 10 feet apart and crawled along at 10 to

15 MPH. Taking the lead, I could only see out the side window, straight down at the yellow line on the edge of the highway. Trouble is like being captive to the elements, not able to see anything ahead.

God does not cause trouble. The very nature of this world leads to difficulties and sufferings. Followers of Jesus have no guarantee of trouble-free living. In reality, when life is easy, spiritual fortitude becomes weak. Strength only comes by exertion.

If complacency towards God sets in, trouble helps you remember not to take the relationship with Him for granted. What better way to start looking for God than when His presence is blinded by trouble?

The promise of Scripture is "God is our refuge and strength, a very present help in trouble." (Psalm 46:1) The Lord declares, "Call upon me in the day of trouble; I will deliver you...." (Psalm 50:15)

When held captive to trouble, call out to God, maintain faith, and you will sense His presence before long.

Moments of temptations

A Scripture verse worth memorizing is, "No temptation has overtaken you that is not common to man. God is faithful, and he will not let you be tempted beyond your ability, but with the temptation he will also provide the way of escape, that you may be able to endure it." (1 Corinthians 10:13)

God is *faithful*—dependable and trustworthy. In other words, God is there. During tempting moments people often question His presence. No believer is left without His help.

The Bible reveals temptations come from sin, self, and the satan. Temptations are designed to *destroy* faith. Followers of Jesus are far from being exempt of temptations and should expect them to occur regularly. Someone diligently walking with God will have the life-giving relationship challenged by the spiritual enemy.

Although temptations in themselves are not sin, they lead to sinning. God knows how to rescue the godly from them all. (2 Peter 2:9)

The compelling force of a temptation only leaves with some form of separation. Sometimes temptations are removed; more often, people must remove themselves from temptations.

God always reveals an escape. Once revealed, there is no time for debate, only obedience. If a person yields to temptation, the Lord was still there and a solution was given, but personal want and temporary weakness won the battle.

When held captive to temptation, run for your life without looking back, exercise faith, and you will sense His presence once again.

Seasons of trials

Temptations rob people of an intimate relationship with God, but testing strengthens the bond. Tests build faith.

School exams are a measurement of knowledge and a means of learning. There is no escaping a test unless a person plans to retake the lesson. No one graduates with *incompletes*.

Many professing faith in Jesus are satisfied with "Incompletes" on their spiritual report card. They are not advancing in Christlikeness.

Temptations come with escapes, while completed tests result in promotion. Divine tests reveal the grandeur of His love and devotion toward you, transforming self-sufficiency into greater reliance upon God.

Job is a classic example of the war between temptations and testing. The devil turned tragedies into trash talk. After losing wealth and health, Job's wife said, "Curse God and die." Friends added,

"You've got sin in your life! Confess what we suspect you're doing wrong." Temptations sometimes occur during a test, causing confusion and debate.

To put an end to his misery, to stop the turmoil and feelings of despair, Job was tempted to deny the grace, mercy and fairness of God. The father of lies wanted him to confess something not true. The devil hoped he would discontinue the test before it was completed.

Terrorizing events have testing purposes. An honest personal assessment leads to a more accurate awareness of God. Job passed his final exam and was promoted to greater blessings.

When held captive to a test, keep walking with the Lord, remain committed to faith, and you will sense His presence in no time.

Periods of tears

Followers of Jesus are familiar with tears. Tears flow in times of joy as well as sorrow.

My administrative assistant in a northwest suburban church near Chicago was easily moved to tears. When the congregation reached a financial goal to expand the facility, tears of joy came. When a phone call arrived at the office of my mother's unexpected death, tears of sorrow flowed freely.

Tears are also associated with salvation:

Tears sometimes stream down the cheeks of someone expressing repentance.

Believers stain altars with tears for the numerous lives needing the divine answer for guilt and hopelessness.

The heavenly host weeps over people who refuse to commit their life to Christ.

The burden of and for the broken causes tears.

The Apostle Paul reminded his friends, "You yourselves know how I lived among you the whole time from the first day that I set foot in Asia, serving the Lord with all humility and with tears...." (Acts 20:18-19)

Weeping can also occur during periods of cruelty and injustice, when God's presence is questioned. The Psalmist wrote, "You have kept count of my tossing; put my tears in your bottle. Are they not in your book? (Psalm 56:8)

Weeping does not always mean the absence of God but sometimes reveals a greater sensitivity to the things touching His heart. A lack of tears can be a sign of indifference.

"Those who sow in tears shall reap with shouts of joy! He who goes out weeping, bearing the seed for sowing, shall come home with shouts of joy, bringing his sheaves with him." (Psalm 126:5-6)

When held captive to tears, find solace in the Lord, abide in faith, and before long you will sense His presence.

WHO IS GOD?

He is YHWH-shammah—the Lord is there. Are you currently feeling captive to trouble, temptation, trial, or tears? Make necessary adjustments, have faith, and regain the sense of His presence.

Take a moment and look around the room where you are reading. Find five things of the same color. In my office, brown got my attention. I was surprised to discover every picture frame has some shade of brown. In fact, the whole room seems very brown to me right now.

When things have something in common, they quickly captivate your attention. Certain objects leap out at you.

At various times in life, God seems strangely

absent but has not disappeared. Something else has your focus and is captivating you. With greater sensitivity for the things of the Lord, you will recognize He is *there*.

CHAPTER ELEVEN

SHEPHERD

The LORD is my shepherd [Jehovah-raah]; I shall not want. He makes me lie down in green pastures. He leads me beside still waters. He restores my soul. He leads me in paths of righteousness for his name's sake. Even though I walk through the valley of the shadow of death, I will fear no evil, for you are with me; your rod and your staff, they comfort me. You prepare a table before me in the presence of my enemies; you anoint my head with oil; my cup overflows. Surely goodness and mercy shall follow me all the days of my life, and I shall dwell in the house of the LORD forever. (Psalm 23)

One of my earlier assignments in church ministry was as the Minister of Youth and Music in Rapid City, South Dakota for an outstanding preacher in the Assemblies of God. Landowners in the western prairies speak of property in terms of sections. A section contains approximately 640 acres.

A family in the church owned several sections, raising grain, cattle, and sheep. They regularly invited my family to spend afternoons and evenings at their home. We loved experiencing the fresh-air living and having a delicious country meal. The place was beautiful; the sunsets were breathtaking.

During one of our visits, the owner wanted to check his flock of sheep and invited me to ride along. We drove for 30 minutes at a fairly high speed, never leaving his property. As soon as the animals noticed his truck, they started coming together. He slowed down, stopped, turned off the engine, opened his door, and began speaking in a calm and loving voice. They immediately approached him.

I then opened the other door and, while slowly walking toward the owner, quietly made a comment. The sheep immediately scattered. The owner's dog gathered them together and herded them back to their shepherd.

Two things highlighted this experience: First, sheep know and are comforted by the voice of their loving owner; they are rightfully fearful of the voice of strangers and quickly flee.

Secondly, sheepdogs do not run interference or take the place of a caring shepherd. They bring the animals to the one who truly watches over them.

People come to the true and loving God only when they recognize His voice, and those working for the Lord should always bring them to Him instead of running interference. He alone is the answer to every need. Anything less is a poor substitute.

The 23rd Psalm describes God as *YHWH-raah*, sometimes translated *rohi*—the Lord our Shepherd. Additional verses give clarity to this aspect of God.

"I am the good shepherd. The good shepherd lays down his life for the sheep.... I am the good shepherd. I know my own and my own know me." (John 10:11, 14)

"He will tend his flock like a shepherd; he will gather the lambs in his arms; he will carry them in his bosom, and gently lead those that are with young." (Isaiah 40:11)

"We your people, the sheep of your pasture, will give thanks to you forever; from generation to generation we will recount your praise." (Psalm 79:13)

What causes thanksgiving and praise to ascend

up to YHWH-raah?

The Lord tends His flock

"As a shepherd seeks out his flock when he is among his sheep that have been scattered, so will I seek out my sheep, and I will rescue them from all places where they have been scattered on a day of clouds and thick darkness." (Ezekiel 34:12)

An old gospel song says, "God will take care of you, through every day, o'er all the way...." Although rarely sung these days, the church needs to be reminded of the lyrics. Created in His image and likeness, God knows all your needs and has set out to meet each and every one of them.

There are three main areas of need:

Physical: At the Garden of Eden, the man and woman rebelled, and the stark nakedness of their action was exposed. God covered the shame of their behavior with a sacrifice—a garment of skin. The covering speaks of physical atonement, which includes attending to tangible needs.

God is concerned about the well-being of your physical life. He seeks to graciously clothe you with goodness, and makes provision for shelter, sustenance, and safety. The natural and material aspects of life are a genuine concern to Him.

Social: In the classic movie "Cast Away", the main character, played by Tom Hanks, is so hungry for companionship that a piece of sporting equipment, a trademark ball, becomes an imaginary friend named "Wilson". People instinctively long for friendship with others.

Following Jesus is divinely and naturally relational. Church gatherings are about connection and interaction; a place where priority is given to engaging God with others.

With entertainment heavily promoted in society, some expect nothing more than a great performance at church. Words like *party*, *fun*, and *good time* are frequently and mistakenly used to describe events and activities. A more accurate depiction of faith and community is "living life together". People can easily thrive without being a spectator of a show, but not without the exchange of love and concern.

Spirit: The body is wasting away but the person continues to live. Jesus promised at His departure to send the Helper, which He did. The Holy Spirit was sent to abide within those who love Jesus, fulfilling every inward longing until eternally satisfied in His presence.

Spiritual interests run high throughout the world, but many look for fulfillment where the Spirit of God cannot be found, in vain philosophies and mystical experiences. His ways are mysterious, not futile or magical. Many pursuing in wrong places come away with poor substitutes and greater disappointments. The human heart is design solely for the Holy Spirit.

Every believer needs the full blessing of the Spirit. He has come to provide overcoming power and gives the means to wholeheartedly follow Jesus. The Lord did not consider the baptism in the Holy Spirit as optional but as part of a divine effort to meet your spiritual needs more completely.

The Lord gives attention to human needs.

The Lord gathers and carries

"For thus says the Lord GOD: Behold, I, I myself will search for my sheep and will seek them out." (Ezekiel 34:11)

The gospel writer records Jesus saying He came to seek and save those who are lost. People are often described as searching for God, yet He pursues until they notice Him.

Comparable behavior is occasionally seen in

social settings. Have you ever witnessed someone positioning themselves in a crowd to be more readily noticed? Similarly, God does not force a personal relationship upon anyone but initiates witnessing opportunities, waiting patiently to be discovered.

The church exists to tell others locally and globally about Jesus. Those telling His story have a very special place in the heart of God. They make it possible for Him to be noticed.

The assignment to make disciples is given to every believer. Disobedience is possible but not without consequences: sin will intensify, and the influence of the church will weaken. If followers of Jesus fail to be involved in the ingathering of people, they are failing God and hurting themselves.

Not only does God gather but He also carries. When people place faith in Him, they are not sent on their way but are graciously held up. He stays with them, lifting them over the difficult hurdles on the pathway of life. He is never too distant for a conversation and a response.

The Lord seeks and carries those who take notice of Him.

The Lord leads and directs

"He leads me beside still waters." (Psalms 23:2)

"For the Lamb in the midst of the throne will be their shepherd, and he will guide them to springs of living water, and God will wipe away every tear from their eyes." (Revelation 7:17)

As sheep in His pasture, you are being led to a refreshing, life-giving source that never runs dry. Although often captivated by the thirst-quenching portion of His promises, remember the One who gives them. He personally directs you on a meaningful and fulfilling pathway.

Elisabeth Elliot tells a story of two adventurers who stopped to see her. They were loaded with equipment for the rainforest east of the Andes. They sought no advice; they just wanted a few phrases to converse with the local people.

She wrote, "Sometimes we come to God as the two adventurers came to me—confident and, we think, well-informed and well-equipped. But has it occurred to us that with all our accumulation of stuff, something is missing?

"What we really ought to have is the Guide Himself. Maps, road signs, a few useful phrases are good things, but infinitely better is Someone who has been there before and knows the way." *

Years ago, I headed up a construction team to help a missionary in South America. No one traveling with me was fluent in Spanish. Our host arranged for an interpreter to help us through the international terminal and bring us to the national terminal. The person failed to show up.

We had to figure out for ourselves how to traverse the various lines and find the next gate, involving moments of uncertainty, confusion, and humor.

While waiting in the national terminal, everyone became hungry. A member of the group knew enough words to provide help. He placed an order for hamburgers, some team members wanted cheese. Those expecting a cheeseburger received their order with a fried egg on top of the meat. We all had a good laugh and ate what was served. The egg-burgers tasted pretty good.

God does not leave you to fend for yourself. He accurately guides and clearly helps.

A television program preceding the 1988 Winter Olympics featured blind skiers being trained for slalom skiing. Paired with sighted skiers, they were taught on the flats how to make right and left turns. When this was mastered, they were taken to the slalom slope. The sighted partners skied beside them shouting, "Left!"—"Right!".

By obeying the commands, they could navigate the course and cross the finish line. They were dependent solely on the words of the sighted skiers.

In this world, you can easily become blind about which way to go. Jesus, the Good Shepherd, longs for you to hear His voice. He will lead and direct you.

WHO IS GOD?

He is YHWH-raah—the Lord our Shepherd. He is the majestic King that leads like a gentle Shepherd. He longs to meet every need, gathering His own and directing their path. Rely solely on the One who abundantly knows the way.

*(Fleming H. Revell, Grand Rapids, MI: A Slow and Certain Light, by Elisabeth Elliot, 1992)

EPILOGUE

LORD GOD

The names of God written in Scripture reveal that He is powerful, personable, and present. He is everlasting and beyond comparison to any and all things, giving abundant provisions for life. He is the victorious healer, sufficiently providing inner peace and tranquility. He is your righteousness.

Additional names recorded in Scripture express other divine qualities:

El-berith—*God of the covenant.* (Judges 9:46) He alone establishes and maintains binding promises.

El-roi—*God who sees me,* or *God of vision.* (Genesis 16:13) No one is ever out of His sight.

YHWH-mekaddesh—*the Lord of hosts.*

(Exodus 31:13) He is King and Ruler over the whole realm of heaven.

Symbolic titles are associated with Him, as well. He is the *Ancient of Days*, active in time and history. (Daniel 7:9) He is the *Rock*, strong and permanent. (Deuteronomy 32:18) He is a *Refuge*, a haven from enemies. (Psalms 9:9) He is a *Fortress*, a defense against foes. (Psalms 18:2) He is a *Shield*, supernatural protection. (Genesis 15:1) He is the *Sun*, the source of light and life. (Psalms 84:1) He is a *Refiner*, molding and shaping purity. (Malachi 3:3)

In the New Testament, He is approached as the *Father*. (Matthew 6:9) He is the *Father of mercies* (2 Corinthians 1:3), the *Father of lights* (James 1:17), and the *Father of glory* (Ephesians 1:17).

The covenant-making Creator is amazing and awesome. Can anyone fully comprehend Him? No! He is as vast as the universe yet wonderfully intimate.

Have you made the Lord God too small in your mind and imagination? When fearful about the future, your thoughts of Him are too small. When anxious about your circumstances, you are placing limits on His abilities.

The God of the Bible is watching over you. He desires to give you loving and personal attention.

There is no such thing as being lost in a crowd. He gives individual oversight to His own and thoroughly addresses every need.

Fulfillment and satisfaction are found solely in a relationship with *Elohim/YHWH*. He is the truly majestic and wonderful Lord God. Place your faith in Him and follow Jesus. The Holy Spirit will come alongside to help and guide.

S. ROBERT MADDOX

WORD STUDY

"YHWH"

The word *YHWH* is the Hebrew name for God revealed to Moses in Exodus. The word consists of a sequence of consonants and is known as the tetragrammaton. The word became regarded as too sacred to be uttered by just anyone. It was used exclusively by the High Priest in the Temple's Holy of Holies on the Day of Atonement—by the holiest person, in the holiest place, on the holiest day.

The tetragrammaton has no vowels, making it impossible for English-speaking people to know how to pronounce the name. So, where did the "a" and "e" come from?

There are three words in scripture for the one Supreme Being: *YHWH* (LORD), *Adonai* (Lord), and *Elohim* (God). To make it possible for most people to pronounce the word YHWH, the first letter of the two other names was inserted, making "*Yahweh*." Although the pronouncement is close in sound to the Hebrew intonations, it is not entirely accurate.

The Hebrew consonants are Yod, Heh, Waw, and Heh. In the letter "H" are vowel inflections that non-agglutinative language groups find difficult to correctly pronounce (English is an analytic language). Latin-speaking scholars replaced the Y, which does not exist in Latin, with an I or a J and the Latinized name became Jehovah (JeHoWaH).

To be true to the main expressions of God recorded in scripture, the tetragrammaton was used throughout this book when giving attention to his personal name.

BONUS FEATURE

GLORY

For unto you is born this day in the city of David a Savior, who is Christ the Lord…. And suddenly there was with the angel a multitude of the heavenly host praising God and saying, "Glory to God in the highest, and on earth peace among those with whom he is pleased!" (Luke 2:11, 13-14)

Over a hundred years ago, the German philosopher Friedrick Nietzsche made the remark that when God dies, culture becomes *weightless*. When God dies in the heart of a nation, the nation loses its strength.

The word "glory" (the Old Testament Hebrew *kabod*, and the New Testament Greek *doxa*) is rooted in the word *heaviness*. The comparable Latin word *dignitas* is the root of the English word "dignity."

People have dignity when something is *weighty* about them.

Only God possesses the eternal weight of glory; He alone is *kabod*. The Old Testament prophet Habakkuk states no idol compares to His glory. They are dumb and speechless, a product of people trusting in themselves and their own ability. (Habakkuk 2:18-20)

Dignity is derived, dependent, and contingent upon God stamping His image and likeness upon you. Scripture conveys this truth: "Now the Lord is the Spirit, and where the Spirit of the Lord is, there is freedom. And we all, with unveiled face, beholding the glory of the Lord, are being transformed into the same image from one degree of glory to another. For this comes from the Lord who is the Spirit." (2 Corinthians 3:17-18)

The Lord's glory has a sense of heavenly *gravity*. During special times of holy stirrings, people are often drawn to their knees. Compelled by the Spirit, they drop to the ground by the gravity-pull of His presence.

"When the priests came out of the Holy Place, a cloud filled the house of the LORD, so that the priests could not stand to minister because of the cloud, for the glory of the LORD filled the house of the LORD. Then Solomon said, 'The LORD has said that he would dwell in thick darkness.'" (1 Kings 8:10-12)

"Behold, the glory of the God of Israel was coming from the east. And the sound of his coming was like the sound of many waters, and the earth shone with his glory. ... And I fell on my face." (Ezekiel 43:2-3)

The prophet Daniel received a divine visitation and, hearing His voice, fell on his face to the ground. (Daniel 10:9)

Revelation 5 records all the creation shouting God's glory and the elders in heaven falling to the ground in worship. (Revelation 5:14)

Note the opposite: First Samuel 4 records a time when Israel thought *lightly* of the Ark of the Covenant, the visible presence of divine glory. They demonstrated a *shallow* relationship with God. A priestly child was born and given the name Ichabod ("no glory") as a testimony of the nation's spiritual *weightlessness*.

The book of Daniel records the Babylonian King Belshazzar irreverently using holy vessels, taken from the Temple, and of a divine finger writing a phrase on a wall, interpreted as, "You have been weighed on the scales and found weightless"—spiritually deficient and personally shallow. (Daniel 5:27)

When people move away from the Lord, they end up hollow. They sense the feeling of *Ichabod*, empty of glory. By being found weightless, life appears meaningless and loses value.

Christ came in order for everyone to become filled with divine *doxa*. Worth and significance come with the glory of the Lord. "Glory to God", the angelic proclamation of Christmas, brings *weight* and *dignity* to people.

Has the present age now entered an era of weightlessness and shallowness? Without divine gravity (*doxa*) not much is required, simply float along with low demands and few expectations.

Some appear motivated today to do only what is minimally expected and nothing more. They want the least amount of obligation and prefer lots of room for failure.

Relationships are also growing increasingly shallow, including with God. Are men and women secretly hoping superficiality will serve as an excuse when standing before Him in the final tribunal? Are they planning to use ignorance as a defense for moral failure and intentional waywardness?

Is the cry of "Ichabod" coming from deep within your soul? Has the finger of God written an inscription on the wall of your heart, "You have been weighed on the scales of divine glory and found weightless?"

Do a personal assessment in three measurable dimensions of spiritual formation. Is there a lack of substance?

Deepening affections

Where does God fit into your ambitions? What drives, motivates, and compels you? Are you passionate about your relationship with Him? Are you deeply concerned for those not knowing Him?

Deep affections have to do with developing pure passions. What do you mean when you acknowledge love for the Lord? Are you talking about a teenage crush, an emotional high that lacks sincerity and can quickly evaporate?

My wife continues to love me, but I hardly resemble the young man she first met. Most of the hair has left and the rest has turned gray. My body has quickly become Rice Krispies, wrinkled with joints that regularly snap, crackle, and pop. Her love is a deep-seated passion for the person within the shell.

The affections people should have for God is revealed in the Biblical narrative of Ruth and Naomi. Ruth says to her mother-in-law, "Where you go I will go; your people will be my people." A relationship with the Lord involves unconditional and personal devotion. Choosing the Lord includes severing compromising ties.

Your affections for God are to come without stipulations, debate, or selfishness. Do you love Him unreservedly? Or do you love Him only to the measure that He heals, mends, gives, or allows for personal wants and demands?

Out of a deep passion comes a deepening relationship with God, a never-ending hunger to linger and dwell in the shelter of the Most High (Psalms 91:1), an intensifying thirst for His plans to be fulfilled.

How weighty are your affections for God? What is the status of your love for Him? Without the weight of deep affections comes a sense of Ichabod, no glory.

Deepening convictions

Without moral principles, people lack dignity. Do fleeting circumstances, momentary moods, and ever-changing trends determine your actions? No one is fit to make good decisions or able to contribute to the wellbeing of others without strong ethical convictions.

Present-day instruction promotes judging experiences and establishing standards using personal preference. More and more people have the conviction to have no convictions. This is the roadway to anarchy. Everyone ends up deprived of core liberty. Individual freedom requires corporate values and assessments.

Bibles are quickly being placed on the shelf of triviality. Yet, divine truth leads to significance.

Prayer has become a *crisis button*, used only when things are falling apart. Praying, however, is designed for regular communication with the One who holds all things together.

Church involvement is perceived as optional. But a satisfying life involves community. Spiritual formation is inadequate and incomplete without others.

Without the weight of deep convictions comes a sense of Ichabod, no glory.

Deepening foundations

Paul gives a clear warning to end-time believers: "For the time is coming when people will not endure sound teaching, but having itching ears they will accumulate for themselves teachers to suit their own passions, and will turn away from listening to the truth and wander off into myths." (2 Timothy 4:3-4)

With the increase of *me-ism* in the world, self-serving spirituality is creeping into the church. Some lifestyles presently promoted have little, if any, Biblical moorings. When seeking solutions for various ills, temporal truth, instead of absolute truth, is more readily pursued.

Vince Lombardi, of Green Bay Packers fame, stood before his team after a loss to an inferior opponent, held up a football and said, "We are going back to the basics. Men, this is a football!" He believed excellence was best achieved by perfecting the basics. Razzle-dazzle, crowd-pleasing, risk-taking plays fill stadiums, but consistent winners perfect the essentials.

Does God need to hold up a Bible before the church and say, "This is infallible Scripture!" Egopleasing, erroneous distortions may excite crowds and possibly draw audiences, but victorious living is only perfected by mastering the fundamentals. How firm is your spiritual foundation?

Do you live the great truths of salvation? Do you stand unwaveringly on issues of righteousness?

Without the weight of deep foundations comes a sense of Ichabod, no glory.

No glory

C.S. Lewis was one of the great Christian writers of the last century. The seven-book series known as The Chronicles of Narnia is full of imagery, communicating Christ-like character. His book Mere Christianity is a *must read* for any serious follower of Jesus. Several of his books have graced my library through the years.

One book I find extremely fascinating is The Great Divorce. Lewis describes an imaginary event, a busload of citizens taking a ride from hell to heaven. One by one, the passengers decide for various reasons (vanity, pride, conceit, narcissism) to get on the bus and return. No one in their right mind would ever choose to go back. The spiritual truths contained in the book are profound.

The full range of imagery is ingenious. When the citizens from hell arrive, they are light, almost weightless and transparent. They are unable to stand on the solid ground of heaven. Walking is so painful that even a blade of grass hurts the sole of their feet.

One person decides to stay and discovers the process of becoming weighty is traumatic, even painful. While being encouraged by others on his personal journey, he remains steadfast and eventually gains substance enough to experience the abundant pleasures of heaven.

In novel form, Lewis communicates heaven is wonderful because of the weightiness of God's glory. The place, however, will prove unpleasant if someone chooses to remain weightless and deficient. Glory is the focus of life and eternity.

Heaven is the longing of the soul, when possessing deep affections, living by deep convictions, and residing on deep foundations. Heaven is being with God and experiencing the full weight of His glory.

May you never become branded Ichabod, absent of divine glory. May you never be weighed on righteous scales and found weightless.

ACKNOWLEDGEMENTS

My life and ministry were overseen by some marvelous statewide leaders. They were a great resource of knowledge, a resonating voice of insight and a reverberating supply of encouragement. If people in responsible positions help shape and mold a keener understanding of divine authority, I have been extremely fortunate by those answerable to God for my ministerial wellbeing. Their love, care, and diligence helped shape the reflections recorded in the pages of this book.

Montana
Bob Brandt

South Dakota
S.H. Peterson, David Nelson, Steve Schaible

North Dakota
Marcus Bakke

Minnesota
Herman Rohde

Illinois
Ernie Moen, Paul Martin, Larry Griswold

Thank you for excellence in leadership.

S. ROBERT MADDOX

ABOUT THE AUTHOR

Bob was born and raised in the Pacific Northwest. While serving in the Armed Forces during the Vietnam era, he met his wife, Brenda. They have lived in seven States and raised their four children mostly in the greater Chicago area. They presently reside in southern Missouri.

His career has been as a church overseer, a college administrator, a church denomination leader, a classroom instructor, an athletic coach, and an international emissary.

Bob is an ordained minister, as well as a nationally accredited high school volleyball coach. He is passionate for all generations to enter a life-changing relationship with God and having a fully integrated life through Christ.

He continues to write, teach, and speak in various settings. To view more of his current reflections, his blogs can be found at bob-maddox.blogspot.com. His other ten books are available online.

BOOKS BY THE AUTHOR

SPIRIT Living, *abundantly following Jesus*

GOD, *who are You? Reflections from the names of God in the Bible*

TEN Words, *Reflections from the Ten Commandments*

BLESSING and battles, *Reflections on the Blessing of God and the Battles of Life*

ACTION, *Reflections from the gospel of Mark*

The **CHURCH**, *Reflections from Paul's letter to the Ephesians*

practical **FAITH**, *Reflections from James' letter to the Church*

pure **LOVE**, *Reflections from John's first letter to followers of Jesus*

COMFORT, *Reflections from Paul's second letter to the Corinthians*

really **READY**, *Reflections from the prophetic book of Daniel*

"I Didn't See What Was Coming!", *LIVING in Christ*

Available in Hardback, Paperback, and eBook editions.